Five Critical Steps to Survive and Prosper in

THE COMING ECONOMIC ICE AGE

By Robert D. McHugh, Ph.D.

D1508780

THOMAS NOBLE
· BOOKS ·

THOMAS NOBLE

· BOOKS ·

Thomas Noble Books
427 N Tatnall Street #90946
Wilmington, DE 19801-2230
636-922-2634

Library of Congress Control Number: 2013946467

ISBN 978-0-9892357-6-1

Printed in the United States of America

Disclaimer

Dr. Robert McHugh is President and CEO of Main Line Investors, Inc., a company registered as an investment advisor in the Commonwealth of Pennsylvania for ten years, and can be reached at www.technicalindicatorindex.com.

The statements, opinions, buy and sell signals, and analyses presented in this book are provided as a general information and education service only. Opinions, estimates, buy and sell signals, and probabilities expressed herein constitute the judgment of the author as of publication of the book and are subject to change without notice. Nothing contained in this book is intended to be, nor shall it be construed as, investment advice, nor is the information to be relied upon in making any investment or other decision.

Prior to making any investment decision, you are advised to consult with your broker, investment advisor, or other appropriate tax or financial professional to determine the suitability of any investment. Neither Main Line Investors, Inc., nor Main Line Economic, LLC, nor Robert D. McHugh shall be responsible or have any liability for investment decisions based on, or the results obtained from, the information provided.

Dedication

*To my beautiful wife, Denise,
and our wonderful children,
Shawna and Buddy.*

Table of Contents

Introduction

There is an economic collapse fast approaching, a calamity that will be known as the first "Great Depression" of the twenty-first century. The economic crisis will be global, affecting all nations including the United States. This book will show you why I see the event coming, how bad it is going to be, when I believe it will begin, and how you can prepare to survive the storm and even prosper. The economic ruination will make the recessions of 2000 through 2002 and 2007 through 2009 look minor, and could be worse than the Great Depression of the 1930s. However, history has shown that with every economic calamity there are new opportunities to create wealth and prosper – if you are prepared. This book will show you those opportunities and how to be positioned to prosper.

Government intervention will not be sufficient to prevent the damage. The Federal Reserve Bank (the Fed) will fail in its attempts to reverse the collapse. Fiscal policy will not fix the problem. In fact, Fed and government actions will make matters worse. My intent is not to scare you but to prepare you and give you five steps to protect your family, protect your wealth, avoid personal bankruptcy, and have the opportunity to prosper. I will share with you where the stock market is headed, where the U.S. dollar is going, what real estate will be doing, and what gold is likely to be worth. These predictions are not clairvoyant, are not fantasy, and are not based on opinion; they are based on what the markets are telling us, the science that studies the language of the markets, and an understanding of the message of the markets right now.

In the past, similar economic collapses have been followed by life-altering political change and world war. That might result again, and that is one of my concerns about what is headed our way. This book will tell you how to prepare for that possibility.

The stock market is a perfect accumulation of all knowledge from everyone everywhere on the planet. Market prices are the net result of predictions made by everyone everywhere about everything. Every time someone buys something such as a stock, they are making a prediction about the future based on their knowledge of the world; their world; new trends; old, irrelevant trends; what is likely to happen and not happen; and their outlook, be it optimistic or pessimistic. Markets can predict their own future. Economies are the sum of all markets. When markets warn of trouble ahead, it comes; and economies suffer. When markets say the future is bright, economic prosperity follows.

The stock market right now is warning of impending danger to itself and therefore to the economy – a danger that is more ominous than we have seen in a century, perhaps centuries. The language of the market is an excellent source for forecasting, one I take very seriously. And you should as well. I describe historic instances when the stock market gave similar warnings, and what followed. You will be convinced, as I am, that we need to prepare for the trouble dead ahead. Those who take the stock market's warning seriously, and prepare, will not only survive but be positioned to prosper.

The good news is that there are steps we can take to mitigate the pain, protect ourselves, and be positioned to grab new wealth-building opportunities. The coming **Economic Ice Age™** can be a blessing instead of a curse. I will show you a conservative portfolio model that will outperform markets and protect your wealth. This is tough stuff, but hard times are being foretold, and as in Noah's day, we need to build our arks. This book will help you do just that.

CHAPTER ONE

The Evidence for Approaching Economic Calamity

How do I know there is an economic collapse fast approaching – a calamity that will be known as the first "Great Depression" of the twenty-first century? This is not opinion, clairvoyant knowledge, doom and gloom for profit's sake, a guess, conjecture, or baseless fear. There is a powerful, reliable, clear message coming from the stock market itself that is rare, but has been observed before and was an accurate warning of economic downturns. The difference this time is that the warning is more ominous than those seen or felt over the past century and that the size of the coming economic calamity is going to be larger than any seen in centuries.

To truly understand this message you need to first understand the science of technical market analysis. ***Technical market analysis*** is the discipline of forecasting the direction of stock, bond, commodity, and currency prices through the study of past market data, primarily price and volume. The underlying thesis is that market price moves are the result of the mass psychology of all investors everywhere, that these price moves form patterns, and that these patterns predict future market price moves. Charts that show these patterns are the pictures that predict future price behavior; they are in essence the language of the markets. Markets are telling us where they are headed next through these pictures and patterns formed over time.

Further, technical market analysis is the working knowledge of the language of the markets. By studying and understanding technical market analysis, we can understand what the markets are telling us about the future of market prices. But you do not need to understand technical market analysis to understand the warning the market is giving at this time. I will show you the pattern and explain it, along with examples from the past when it appeared on a smaller scale.

Stock market price action is a forecaster of economic activity. If stocks slide, intuitively one would think it means an economic slowdown is coming. If stocks rise, intuitively one would think it means economic prosperity is coming. However, it's not so simple. If a rise or fall in stock prices completes a larger pattern, the nature of the pattern is the true predictor of future economic activity, not the price trend itself. The good news is that if we can predict where market prices are headed based on patterns forming in those markets, we can also predict whether the economy is headed into a period of boom, bust, or something in between. Market patterns are a lot like weather patterns; once we spot them we can predict whether sunshine or storms are coming, when, and how intense the weather will be.

While there are many tools used in technical market analysis, and many patterns and indicators that are helpful in predicting the future of markets and economies, some messages of the market are clearer, more dramatic, and more telling than others. Some patterns are short-term-focused, some are only more or less reliable, and some are not associated with broader-picture economic trends; they are helpful for short-term trading or for playing weekly or monthly stock trends.

There is a big-picture stock market pattern completing now that is so huge, so powerful, so clear, and which has such important historical and predictive significance to global economies that it must be seen, understood, and respected. It is a pattern that has appeared eight times over the past century, warning of coming stock market declines and subsequent economic downturns with amazing predictive accuracy. It is a *big-boy* pattern, a business-cycle pattern, an impact pattern. But this time even more significant is its size. It is a pattern that has taken two decades to form, meaning it forecasts a market and economic downturn of Biblical proportions. This pattern is much larger than any seen in the past century, and its structure is textbook perfect. It is a heavy-duty warning to the world from the markets that economic calamity is coming, and unfortunately, because the pattern is nearly complete, it is fast approaching.

The pattern is called a *broadening top* or *megaphone* pattern. It shows up best in the Dow Industrials stock index, but also appears in the Dow Transportation index as well as the Standard & Poor's 500. I dub it the **Jaws of Death™** pattern, because every time it rears its ugly head, a massive stock market decline follows, with an intense recession or depression as the result. It is a picture that resembles a shark's massive open jaws ready to devour its prey. It is an ominous stock market pattern, and the market is warning us in no uncertain terms to watch out, that danger is coming.

Let's take a look at this pattern as of June 30, 2013:

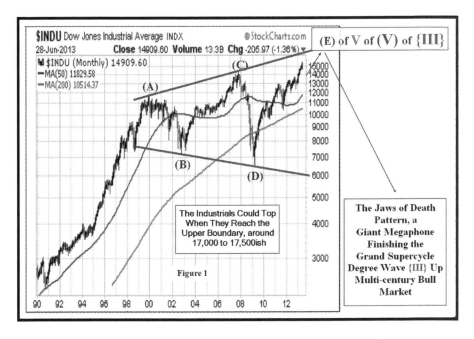

Figure 1

(E) of V of (V) of {III}

The Industrials Could Top When They Reach the Upper Boundary, around 17,000 to 17,500ish

The Jaws of Death Pattern, a Giant Megaphone Finishing the Grand Supercycle Degree Wave {III} Up Multi-century Bull Market

The chart shows a pattern of two symmetrical boundary lines, each defined by two turn points – points (A) and (C) for the top boundary and points (B) and (D) for the bottom boundary. The degree of slope of the upper and lower boundary lines is identical, but in reverse, which is a key characteristic of the pattern, adding to its credibility and increasing the probability that its forecast will prove to be accurate. Because each boundary line is defined by at least two plot points, the positioning of the lines is precise, making the pattern valid. No guessing, no subjective plotting here.

Such megaphone top patterns require five waves of opposing price action. Stocks are finishing the fifth and final move now, from point (D) to point (E). The market has defined this pattern, not me. The market is speaking. If there is any good news, it is that the final wave (E) requires more time – more upside in stock prices – because prices almost always rise to the upper boundary line for its final point (E). The chart shows that as this book is being written, the Dow Industrials have not yet reached the upper boundary line. This gives us preparation time and, for those in the stock market, a bit more profit return before prices plunge and it's time to position ourselves for the changes that are coming. When this pattern appears as a top in the stock market, not a bottom, it tells us a plunge is inevitably coming. The chart tells us the Industrials could rally to new all-time highs, then over the course of several years plunge down below 5,000 – drop maybe as much as 90 percent. The impact on the economy will be devastating.

To gain a proper respect for the above pattern and for the warning the market is providing, we need to take a look at when this pattern has appeared over the past century, what stock prices did once the pattern finished, and what the result was for the economy. Let's begin that study.

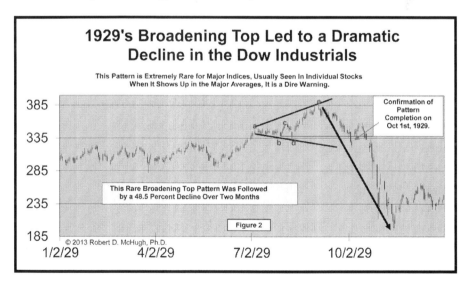

The above chart reveals that the Jaws of Death pattern showed up just before the stock market crash of 1929, which was followed by the twentieth century's Great Depression. The Great Depression led to World War II. This pattern formed over three months. The current pattern we are concerned with has been in formation for over twenty years. The 1929 Jaws of Death pattern led to a 48.5 percent stock market plunge immediately after it finished. Impressive. Was it coincidence? No.

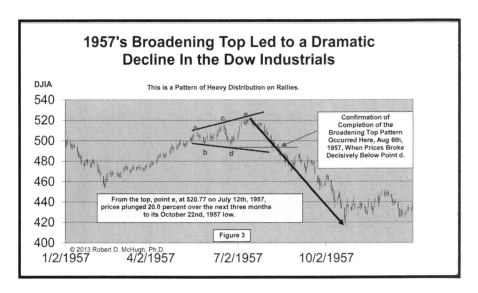

The second time it showed up was in 1957. The pattern took three months to form, and as soon as it finished (note that stocks topped precisely at the upper boundary in their wave e final rally move) the Industrials plunged 20 percent over the next three months. This stock market plunge led to a recession which led to the election of John F. Kennedy. The Cuban Missile Crisis and escalation of the cold war followed.

The third time this pattern showed up was 1965 through 1966. This was a larger pattern, taking a year to form, but slightly less perfect than what we are seeing now, as its fourth wave – its d wave – failed to drop to the bottom boundary. Still, the market did provide two pivot points to draw the bottom boundary with an identical, but inverse, slope to its upper boundary, making the pattern valid. The result? Prices plunged 26.5 percent as soon as its final wave e finished at the top of its upper boundary. The plunge lasted longer than previous plunges because the pattern took longer to form. The subsequent plunge lasted six months. The economic result was another recession and an escalation of the Vietnam War. Isn't it interesting that the dominos fall in the same pattern: First the Jaws of Death appears, then markets plunge, then economies fall into either recession or depression, then war. Amazing.

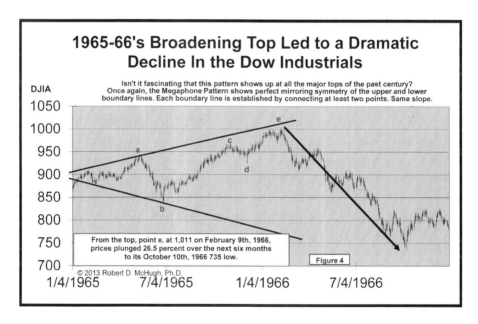

1965-66's Broadening Top Led to a Dramatic Decline In the Dow Industrials

Isn't it fascinating that this pattern shows up at all the major tops of the past century? Once again, the Megaphone Pattern shows perfect mirroring symmetry of the upper and lower boundary lines. Each boundary line is established by connecting at least two points. Same slope.

DJIA

From the top, point e, at 1,011 on February 9th, 1966, prices plunged 26.5 percent over the next six months to its October 10th, 1966 735 low.

Figure 4

© 2013 Robert D. McHugh, Ph.D.

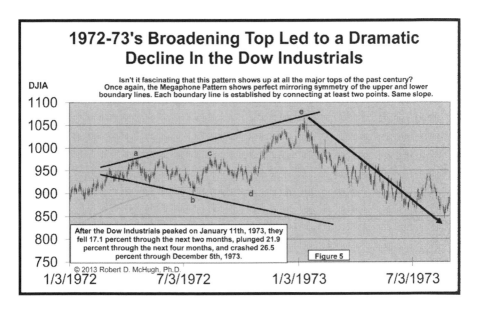

1972-73's Broadening Top Led to a Dramatic Decline In the Dow Industrials

DJIA

Isn't it fascinating that this pattern shows up at all the major tops of the past century? Once again, the Megaphone Pattern shows perfect mirroring symmetry of the upper and lower boundary lines. Each boundary line is established by connecting at least two points. Same slope.

After the Dow Industrials peaked on January 11th, 1973, they fell 17.1 percent through the next two months, plunged 21.9 percent through the next four months, and crashed 26.5 percent through December 5th, 1973.

Figure 5

© 2013 Robert D. McHugh, Ph.D.

1100
1050
1000
950
900
850
800
750

1/3/1972   7/3/1972   1/3/1973   7/3/1973

Next came the 1972 through 1973 Jaws of Death pattern. This pattern took a year to form and had a less-than-perfect pattern in that waves c and d failed to touch their respective upper and lower boundaries. However, the market provided at least two defining pivot points for drawing symmetrical, equal, but opposite sloping trend lines, so the pattern was valid. The result was a 26.5 percent plunge in the Dow Industrials over the subsequent year, with an immediate plunge of 21.9 percent over the next four months. Nixon resigned from office shortly after the plunge, and a significant recession gripped the economy and lasted deep into the decade, with oil shortages plaguing world economies, and economic war with OPEC oil-producing nations.

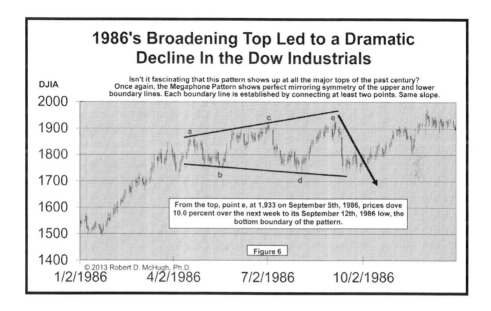

1986's Broadening Top Led to a Dramatic Decline In the Dow Industrials

Isn't it fascinating that this pattern shows up at all the major tops of the past century? Once again, the Megaphone Pattern shows perfect mirroring symmetry of the upper and lower boundary lines. Each boundary line is established by connecting at least two points. Same slope.

From the top, point e, at 1,933 on September 5th, 1986, prices dove 10.0 percent over the next week to its September 12th, 1986 low, the bottom boundary of the pattern.

Figure 6

© 2013 Robert D. McHugh, Ph.D.

DJIA: 2000, 1900, 1800, 1700, 1600, 1500, 1400

1/2/1986   4/2/1986   7/2/1986   10/2/1986

In 1986 we saw the pattern again. This pattern was textbook perfect, and only took three months to form. The resultant decline was relatively mild; markets fell only 10 percent and fell over a very short period of time before recovering. Iran Contra political issues followed, and markets were setting up for the coming smash-up in October of 1987.

Yes, the pattern appeared again in 1987, warning of one of the worst stock market crashes of all time. I remember that crash. For those of you too young to have lived through it, let me tell you it was terrifying. This Jaws of Death pattern only took three months to form, but the second it finished the Industrials plunged 41 percent over the next two months. The wipeout was broad-based. An economic recession followed, lasting into the early 1990s. The recession was featured and fed by a reluctance on the part of banks to lend money. Bill Clinton beat George Herbert Bush in 1992 on the mantra "It's the economy, Stupid." The 1987 Jaws of Death pattern was followed by the first Iraq war. The

U.S. government established the now infamous Plunge Protection Team to try to prevent future stock market crashes.

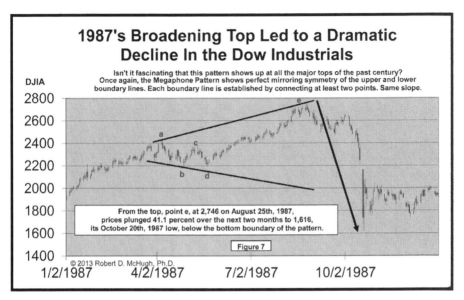

1987's Broadening Top Led to a Dramatic Decline In the Dow Industrials

Isn't it fascinating that this pattern shows up at all the major tops of the past century? Once again, the Megaphone Pattern shows perfect mirroring symmetry of the upper and lower boundary lines. Each boundary line is established by connecting at least two points. Same slope.

From the top, point e, at 2,746 on August 25th, 1987, prices plunged 41.1 percent over the next two months to 1,616, its October 20th, 1987 low, below the bottom boundary of the pattern.

Figure 7

© 2013 Robert D. McHugh, Ph.D.

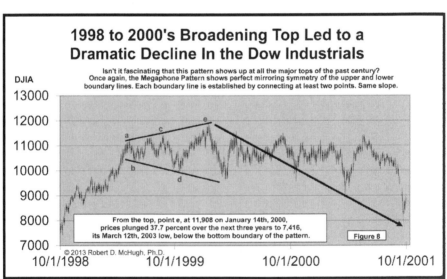

1998 to 2000's Broadening Top Led to a Dramatic Decline In the Dow Industrials

Isn't it fascinating that this pattern shows up at all the major tops of the past century? Once again, the Megaphone Pattern shows perfect mirroring symmetry of the upper and lower boundary lines. Each boundary line is established by connecting at least two points. Same slope.

From the top, point e, at 11,908 on January 14th, 2000, prices plunged 37.7 percent over the next three years to 7,416, its March 12th, 2003 low, below the bottom boundary of the pattern.

Figure 8

© 2013 Robert D. McHugh, Ph.D.

The next time we saw the pattern was from 1998 through 1999. It took about a year to complete, and formed a nice textbook pattern. This pattern demonstrates the point that the longer the Jaws of Death pattern takes to form, the longer and deeper the resultant market collapse and economic decline. This pattern was immediately followed by a stock market plunge of over 20 percent over several months. But worse, it led to a continuous stock market plunge lasting over two years. By the time the plunge was over, stocks had lost 50 percent of their value. A severe recession followed this Jaws of Death pattern, one that lasted several years. It came just before the Y2K fears and was followed by the 911 World Trade Center and Pentagon terrorist attacks and the second Iraq war. This pattern is on a smaller scale but similar to what we see finishing now. It gives us an idea of the kind of trouble coming our way. But again, the scale and magnitude of the current Jaws of Death pattern warns us that the coming plunge and economic calamity will be far worse.

Get the picture? Market meltdown, then economic downturns, then wars.

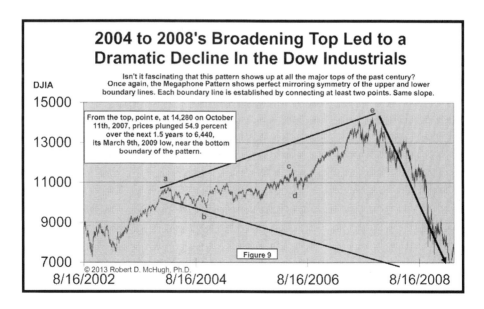

The next and most recent time we see the pattern is from 2004 through 2008. This was a large pattern, taking five years to form. While the c and d points don't fall precisely on the upper and lower boundary lines, the pattern has at least two pivot points for drawing symmetrical upper and lower boundary lines, so it is valid. It sure was right, wasn't it? It warned us that a massive decline was coming. As soon as this pattern finished in October of 2007, stocks plunged over 50 percent from October 2007 through March 2009, a two-and-a-half-year stock market plunge. It can be argued that the economy still has not recovered from this recession. The result is what many call the Great Recession. The real estate market collapsed and has not recovered. Monetary inflation has increased the cost of living dramatically, and unemployment has doubled. Wall Street firms collapsed during this economic disaster.

The Jaws of Death pattern I currently have my eyes focused on (the first chart shown at the beginning of this chapter) overlaps two of these prior patterns. That is how huge it is. The current pattern is textbook perfect. Its point (C) and (D) pivot turns have landed precisely on the upper and lower boundary lines. The lines are perfectly symmetrical. The slopes are the same. This is one very dangerous pattern. It tells us that the Industrials will rise to the upper boundary to finish their wave '(E) rally at about 17,000 to 17,500 sometime in 2014 or 2015. (These levels and dates depend on how fast prices ascend. The slower they rise, the higher they will go and the longer it will take for the pattern to complete, because prices are chasing a rising target since the upper boundary of the Jaws of Death pattern is also rising.) A massive stock market plunge will immediately follow, one that lasts several years – maybe seven to ten years (because this pattern has taken two decades to form) – to be accompanied by economic events that destroy the economy and likely lead to a great depression and an eventual world war.

It is impossible to predict precisely what economic events will transpire or what specific economic problems will manifest, but they will be significant. They could be followed by a terrible war and perhaps political changes we cannot even begin to envision. This Jaws of Death pattern forecasts an Armageddon. Will it be *an* Armageddon or *the* Armageddon predicted in the Bible? There is no way to know. But there will be an end to the calamity eventually, and there will be a return to prosperity, and there will be wealth-building opportunities during and after this coming tribulation period ends.

How do we prepare? Read on.

CHAPTER TWO

How Devastating Will This Coming Economic Collapse Be in Relation to Other Past Economic Declines?

To get an idea of how widespread and deep this collapse is going to be, we want to take a look at an historic chart that maps past declines and labels the forthcoming storm. There is a tool we use to map how the coming collapse fits into history, and which provides perspective on its expected severity.

Before I unveil this chart, let's cover one of the key branches of technical market analysis that I use to map the coming decline. This branch of technical market analysis is Elliott Wave analysis. I am going to oversimplify my explanation of this analysis because the point of this book is not to teach Elliott Wave Theory but to give you a thumbnail sketch so you can understand the map and the degree of severity of the coming decline.

Markets form maps – maps of where they have been and maps of where they are going. Markets are fluid, dynamic, and constantly in motion. They are on journeys, traveling to destinations – up, down, or sideways. By mapping markets and labeling key refueling points and rest stops along their journeys we can start to figure out where they are headed. We can determine whether this is going to be a long journey, a fast journey, or a direct journey. Or we can draw conclusions that suggest that markets are embarking on short, slow, or scenic-route paths. What an incredible advantage *mapping* can provide traders and investors!

Ralph N. Elliott, the founder of Elliott Wave analysis, was an accountant by trade who, in the 1930s, noted that stock market prices form repetitive patterns he called waves. Think of a wave as one leg of a journey – the distance you travel between rest stops. When Elliott became quite ill, he took that bedridden opportunity to study the Dow Jones averages since 1896 when Charles Dow first defined the Industrial and Transportation averages. The result of Elliott's studies was his origination of the Elliott Wave Theory. His body of work was expanded on through the years by such noted technical analysts as A. Hamilton Bolton of the Bank Credit Analyst, A.J. Frost, Richard Russell, Robert R. Prechter Jr., Glenn Neely, and Zoran Gayer. At Main Line Investors, Inc., where I am President, CEO, and Editor, we provide Elliott Wave mapping for major stock, bond, precious metals, and energy markets in newsletters we publish at **www.technicalindicatorindex.com**. We find Elliott Wave mapping incredibly useful.

Elliott Wave Theory is a measure of mass human activity as applied most commonly to the financial markets, although evidence is being gathered by **Robert Prechter** that shows that the theory applies to *socio* patterns as well (see his book *The Wave Principle of Human Social Behavior and the New Science of Socionomics*, New Classics Library, 1999). Elliott Wave confirms what God said through the writer of Ecclesiastes: **"That which has been is that which will be, and that which has been done is that which will be done."** The issue here is of cycles. All of nature repeats itself, which is especially true of markets. It is as if the journeys that markets take are around a sphere and eventually they get back to where they started. And if the journey is long enough they embark on another spherical trip. **These repetitive patterns can be recognized and, to some degree of success, anticipated.**

In a nutshell Elliott Wave Theory goes like this: **Markets reflect all information and all knowledge available to man. They have a language of their own and communicate where they are headed next.** Elliott Wave Theory is one of many languages markets use to tell us where they are moving. The nice thing is that markets are only going one place at a time, and yet they shout their intentions using many dialects all at the same time. So it is not just one language we want to learn, but many. While one language suffices because the market speaks in a harmonious cacophony, it says the same thing many different ways. If you know only one or two languages, but not all of them, you can still understand where markets are headed next over short-term, intermediate-term, and long-term horizons. A short-term journey might take detours, as if you were headed to Los Angeles from New York but had to stop first in Boston to pick up friends, then head to North Carolina for supplies, then to Chicago for some other reason before finally realizing your long-term goal of reaching Los Angeles. As a trader, over the short run, I would like to know where these pit stops are going to be. As an investor with a longer time horizon, I am content to know the ultimate destination and not so worried about the stops along the way. The key questions are whether market prices are going higher or lower, how high or low they are going, and when.

Market moves are not reactive to news announcements but rather independent of news. **News comes as a result of the position of the Elliott Waves – the psychological state of mankind at that particular time.** How news is interpreted depends on the wave. If the wave formation indicates a bullish move is in progress, bad news will be ignored or reacted to in a positive wave; that is, markets will go up anyway. And if the wave pattern is bearish, good news will be ignored or reacted to negatively – markets will sell off. Thus **it is helpful to** investors to be aware of the Elliott Wave position markets find themselves in and which wave pattern is expected to arrive next.

Using the stock market as an example, in Elliott Wave Theory equity prices move up or down *impulsively* with the primary trend. These impulsive (dramatic) moves come in stair-step fashion, five waves at a time. Waves 1, 3, and 5 progress and waves 2 and 4 regress (retrace or correct). The total move in the direction of the primary trend progresses because the sum of waves 1, 3, and 5 exceeds the sum of waves 2 and 4. **Waves 1, 3, and 5 move in the direction of the primary trend (the ultimate destination for the trip), while waves 2 and 4 can either move in the opposite direction or sideways.**

There are five-wave counts at smaller degree inside each of waves 1, 3, and 5. There are three-wave counts at smaller degree inside each wave 2 and 4. Think of a basketball team. While it is moving impulsively toward its basket, there are five subcomponent parts of the team – the five players that make up the team. If you stand far away from that basketball team, say half a mile above the stadium, it might look like one large blob moving from one end of the court to the other. However, as you get closer to the game, you see that the large blob is really five separate people moving in harmony in the same direction.

The five-wave counts are marked by numbers 1 through 5. The three-wave counts are marked by letters A, B, and C. It is as if the roads that take us toward our destination are marked with numbers and those that backtrack are marked with letters. Highway #1 takes us closer to Los Angeles from New York, whereas highway A takes us backwards to Boston to pick up a passenger. Inside the sub-waves A and C are five-wave sub-waves of yet even smaller degree. Inside the B-wave is a set of three sub-waves.

To recap, **waves 1, 3, 5, A, and C are themselves made up of five lower degree waves. Waves 2, 4, and B are built from smaller degree three-wave patterns. Waves 1, 3, 5, A and C push the direction of prices forward and waves 2, 4, and B correct or reverse the progress of the other waves**. An exception is when a wave 5 occurs inside a *triangle*; then it will have a three-wave subset. Sometimes wave A has a three-wave subset, not a five-wave subset; for example, when it is part of a flat 3-3-5 pattern.

Degrees of waves are distinguished based on the time period they cover. Very-long-term waves can cover hundreds of years, such as *Grand Supercycle* degree waves (which is what will conclude once this Jaws of Death pattern finishes). Very-short-term waves might cover only a few weeks, or days. Elliott Waves can even be broken down and identified intraday by hour or minute. Think of a tree. Each tree limb has a subset of branches which has a subset of smaller branches, each of which has its own subset of very small branches, and so on.

The nice thing about this Elliott Wave language of markets is that it comes with definable and reliable rules. Markets move in waves according to rules. Why? Because this is how the group psychology of mankind operates. There are opposing forces that force backward and forward moves in a pattern that keeps everything orderly, sort of like the planets orbiting around the sun. The planets do not spin out of control leaving the sun's orbit to be cast into some faraway galaxy. There are rules to the physics of orbiting planets and gravitational and centrifugal forces at work to keep things as they are. Same thing for markets. It is the Elliott Wave language, or rules, that helps us understand the orbits of markets around our globe, so to speak.

There are certain rules that must not be violated for an accurate Elliott Wave count. Think of it this way. If you are going to learn English so you can understand what someone is saying to you in English, you must learn the rules of that language so it makes sense. If you violate those rules, nobody will understand you. In the same way, if you are going to understand what markets are saying in the Elliott Wave language, you need to understand and follow the rules.

There are three cardinal rules that must be followed for an accurate Elliott Wave count: 1) Wave 2, when it corrects wave 1, can never move prices back beyond the starting point of wave 1. 2) Wave 3 can never be the shortest wave. 3) Wave 4 must never enter the price territory of the same degree wave 1. If any of these rules are violated, the Elliott Wave count is wrong and it is a good bet you are not going to know what the market is telling you about where it is headed and approximately when.

In addition to rules, it is extremely helpful to know the different personalities of each wave. Knowing personalities typical to each wave can sometimes clue you in as to where you are in the count when it is otherwise unclear. If you are traveling from New York to Los Angeles and all around you is a wide-open desert, it is a good bet you are somewhere in Arizona or New Mexico. You get a sense of your whereabouts in relation to the ultimate destination. Arizona and New Mexico have different geographic personalities than say Pennsylvania and Kansas. I'll cover just a few of these wave personalities that I've noticed over the years:

1) Wave 3s are usually (not always) the most dramatic, most powerful, and extend the farthest. Usually. They usually show panic buying or selling where you see prices move almost vertically. Or, if prices move over long periods of

time without corrections, oftentimes it means they are in a wave 3 of some degree. It might be a wave 3 inside a higher degree wave 1, 3, 5, A, or C. This is useful because it means the odds are high that prices will move farther in that same direction before reversing. The impulsive move is not yet over.

2) Ending diagonal patterns (rising bearish or declining bullish wedges) are often seen in wave 5s. These have a subset of five waves, each with its own subset of three waves. This is useful because it tells us the move is nearing its end and a reversal in price direction is approaching.

3) Wave 2s often reverse so sharply, and retrace so much of the previous wave 1's move, that it confuses the Elliottician as to whether in fact the trend has really changed or not. Retracements of as much as 61.8 percent (phi) or 78.6 percent (the square root of phi) are not uncommon in wave 2s.

Note: The mathematical value phi (Φ) is often seen in nature, art, and architecture. It is a number that lends a sense of proper perspective to the eye. For example, a picture frame looks best if one side has a phi relationship to its contiguous side. In other words, the picture frame will seem to have its most pleasant appearance if the ratio of the top side's length to the right side's length is a 61.8 to 38.2 (1.0 minus 61.8) ratio.

4) Wave 4s are often lackluster and more sideways or choppy than 2s (but not always). They often form triangular patterns. Wave Bs often behave like wave 4s – complex, sideways, triangles, lots of oscillations.

Let's take another look at the Jaws of Death pattern chart over the past two decades. This time we will focus on the Elliott Wave mapping.

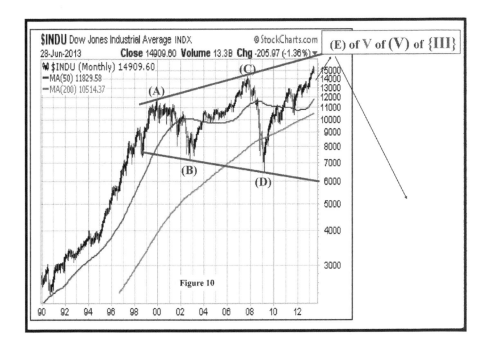

Figure 10

The Jaws of Death pattern is mapped above. It has formed over the past twenty-three years. The Elliott Wave labeling shows an *expanding topping wedge*, also known as a broadening top, or megaphone top, marking the end of several progressive waves of varying time degrees. The pattern is a five-wave move, which is textbook. Each pivot point is marked by a capital letter corresponding to the conclusion of the wave. Four of the required five waves are complete, and the final wave [E] rally leg needs another push higher to the top boundary line to finish the pattern.

I show several annotations in the box at the upper right. Each one is the conclusion of a wave of larger degree than its predecessor. In other words, this pattern is coming at a time of confluence, when (E) will finish the rally from March 2009, when it will also finish the rally for a larger degree (named a *Cycle* degree) wave V from 1974, when it will also finish the rally for an even larger degree (named a *Supercycle* degree) wave (V) from 1932, and finally it will also finish a multi-century rally for one of the largest rally waves on historic record, a *Grand Supercycle* degree wave {III} from the 1700s. Following is the Big Picture Elliott Wave Long-term Count chart showing these degrees of wave trends for the Industrials from 1900 to 2013:

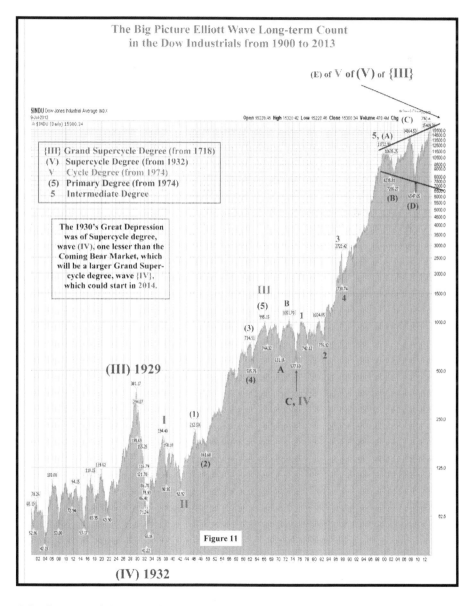

(I thank www.stockcharts.com for allowing me to reprint the chart; annotations are my addition.)

Think about this. The pattern above will be completing four major degrees of market rallying trends dating back centuries for the Grand Supercycle degree {III}. It means that next will come Grand Supercycle degree wave {IV} down, a massive decline in the context of wave degrees. Grand Supercycle degree {IV} down will be correcting a multi-century rise in stock prices (and, ergo, economic activity). We are now about to go into the equivalent of an **Economic Ice Age,** one that could last a very long time or, if it is relatively brief, say seven to ten years, be severe in depth and scope. How do we know? Because one characteristic of Elliott Wave mapping is that waves need to be in proportion to other waves in common degree price movements. If the coming market decline is correcting a Grand Supercycle degree rally that took centuries, it cannot be mild; it has to be severe in either time, depth of decline, or both.

So the answer to the question this chapter raises is yes, the coming economic decline is going to be severe. But again, please keep in mind that you have a little time to prepare; that those who have prepared for disasters in the past, be they economic declines, hurricane warnings, or foreknowledge of disease epidemics, have been able to survive, see opportunities, and be in a position to actually benefit personally. For example, after the U.S. Civil War, during reconstruction, you could have started a lumber company and made a fortune supplying lumber. If you had seen the war coming, you could have supplied the cavalry with horses. You could have accumulated gold and silver in case the Confederate or Union currency became worthless should your side lose the war. One side was going to see its currency become worthless; holding precious metals would have paid off.

Will this coming Economic Ice Age be worse than the stock market crash of 1929 and the subsequent Great Depression of the 1930s? Yes, because that bear market was a degree smaller than the degree this coming bear market will be. That depression was of Supercycle degree. This coming economic collapse will be of a larger Grand Supercycle degree.

The above big-picture long-term chart places all the economic downturns of the past century in perspective with the downturn that is coming. It is in logarithmic scale. This 112-year pictorial view of the markets is fascinating because it allows us to put into perspective the depth of the economic trauma that is coming.

Another interesting perspective to consider is that the stock market crash of 1987, which was turbulent but relatively brief, was merely an intermediate-degree wave 4 decline, four degrees smaller than what we are about to encounter. The recession from the mid-1960s to the late 1970s was merely a Cycle degree wave IV down, which is two degrees of trend less than what we are about to experience.

The coming economic calamity will likely be of such magnitude as to change the political landscape, the economic policy landscape, and the social landscape as we know it. We are already seeing subtle changes toward more government intervention, more government control, and less free-market capitalism. Will this usher in some form of totalitarianism? Well, let's put it this way: Economic crises lead to wars, and during both we certainly do not see less government, we see more. Lincoln threw out the Writ of Habeas Corpus (the right to be brought before a court if accused of a crime, to protect a citizen who has been falsely accused from being detained in prison without sufficient cause or evidence) during the Civil War. The Confederate states seceded and started their own currency, and war broke out as a result of the economic recession of the 1850s. During the Great Depression of the 1930s we saw a president run for four terms; the internment of Asian Americans, which was essentially racial profiling; and government establishment of social programs. The crash of 1987 resulted in the creation of the Plunge Protection Team, which has since birthed four *quantitative easing* programs from the Fed, printing money and handing it to Wall Street asymmetrically. These were unheard-of practices before the crises. In chapter four we will study the likelihood that a major war will accompany this coming Economic Ice Age.

CHAPTER THREE

When Will the Coming Economic Ice Age Begin?

There is an old adage that goes: "Markets always move where they are supposed to, just not necessarily when."

That applies a little bit to the Jaws of Death pattern. There are at least three possible scenarios for the path the market can take to finish the Jaws of Death pattern from where it sits as this book is being written. Each scenario means a different date for the pattern to complete, meaning a different date when the market will start a lengthy plunge and the coming Economic Ice Age will begin. This chapter is a bit technical, so I will do my best to bring it down to an understandable level. Let's explore the timing for each completion scenario.

First of all, this is a two-decade pattern – one of the largest ever. So it is incredible to realize that it is finishing its final leg now. We sit at an historic juncture. The Jaws of Death pattern is completing a multi-century Grand Supercycle degree wave {III} rally. It will be finished when it reaches its upper boundary. That is what history teaches us. All the major Jaws of Death patterns over the past century led to strong declines, and seven out of eight saw their final rally leg precisely reach the upper boundary (only 1986's final wave did not reach the upper boundary, but it came very close). So it is safe to say that the current Jaws of Death pattern will end when prices reach that upper boundary.

Further, once prices reach that upper boundary, they do not rise above that boundary. That is when the top arrives, and the subsequent decline begins.

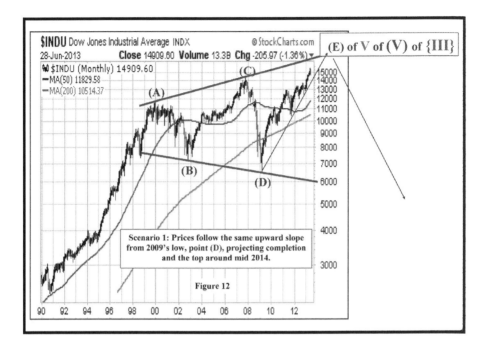

Scenario 1: In the chart above we see that if the slope of the rally from March 2009 remains the same, and we project a continuation of that slope (shown by the rising arrow), then the pattern should finish by mid-2014, with the Industrials rising to about 17,000 to 17,500. This is a logical projection and the highest probability scenario because the slope line also serves as a trend-line with five touch points. The market is telling us that this path – this slope line – is important. The more touch points a trend-line has without prices falling below that trend-line, the greater the probability that prices will continue to follow the path denoted by that trend-line.

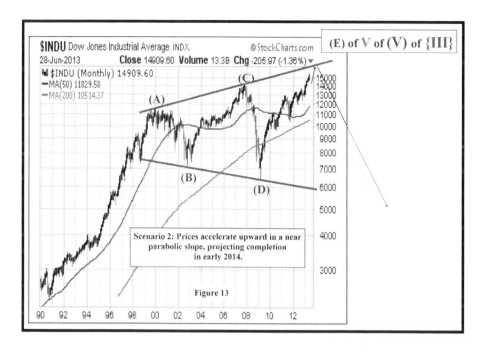

Figure 13

Scenario 2: It is possible that the final flight – the path prices take to finish this pattern by reaching their upper boundary line – will change its slope in its final ascension. It could go parabolic – a sharp, nearly vertical rally. That type of rally often occurs just before crashes. When we see stock prices rise almost vertically, the odds are high that what goes up will go down, like a baseball tossed high overhead. They are going to plunge back down hard. The above demonstrates that possibility. In this scenario the top could occur sometime in early 2014, with the Industrials reaching about 16,500 to 17,000, then free-falling in what would be a kick-off event to the Economic Ice Age, **a stock market crash**. This is the worst-case scenario, not allowing us much time to prepare, and beginning with a crash. This scenario would imply that some horrific news event will accompany the start of the collapse. The good news is that this is not the highest probability scenario for when trouble begins.

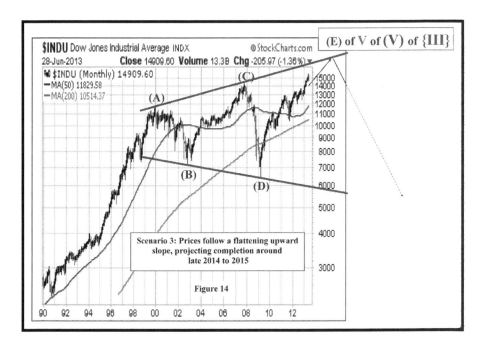

Figure 14

Scenario 3: It is possible that the last rally leg for this pattern will be a more gradual, time-consuming ascension, dragging out this pattern another year or eighteen months. It could be due to continued uncertainty about the ability of government intervention policies to stimulate the economy, or possibly more political gridlock, both of which could have the effect of freezing markets, slowing buying, and delaying completion of this pattern and the start of the economic collapse. The above demonstrates that possibility. In this case the top could occur sometime in late 2014 or even as late as 2015, with the Industrials reaching about 17,500 to 18,000. This scenario would be a blessing, giving us more time to prepare for the coming economic collapse.

We should hope for the best while preparing for the worst.

We will know when the Economic Ice Age begins because that will be when this Jaws of Death price pattern completes. But we have another technical market analysis tool that confirms when the coming Economic Ice Age will begin. I call it the **Primary Trend Indicator™, or PTI.** It is currently on a long-term buy signal. The next time it generates a sell signal, we will have confirmation that the Jaws of Death pattern is finished and the next great bear market and economic depression has started. Let's take a look at this indicator.

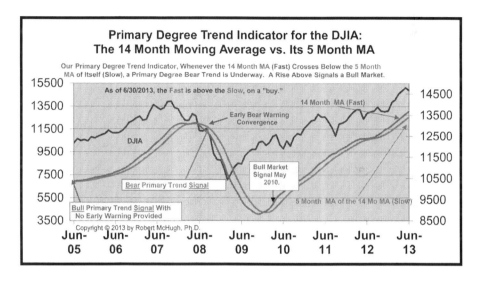

The above chart updates our PTI (the trend that is of large degree and within which all short-term trends operate) as of June 30th, 2013. We cover this as well as the short-term trends in our daily market reports at **www.technicalindicatorindex.com.**

Here is how the PTI works: One of the tools we have in our arsenal to identify the status of a primary trend is a simple analysis of the fourteen-month moving average (MA) versus a slower-moving average calculation – the five-month MA of the fourteen-month MA. **We require a five-month MA of the spread between the *fast* and *slow* to reverse in a new direction for three consecutive months in order to declare that a new primary trend – a new multi-year trend – is underway. There have been only four signal changes since**

1997, so this tool is useful for long-term investors, as it filters out the noise of up and down short-term trends, keeping us focused on the significance of the primary trend – the ultimate price objective that markets are working toward.

How well has this indicator performed in identifying new long-term trends in the stock market? It has been terrific at identifying multi-year trends, both up and down. Here are the past four signals and the size of the stock market move from the point of the signal until the primary trend exhausted itself:

It triggered a sell near the start of primary-degree wave (4) down, on March 31st, 2001, with the Dow Industrials closing at 9,879. What followed was a two-and-a-half-year, **2,682 point, 27 percent drop** in the Industrials into the wave (4) bottom on October 10th, 2002, at 7,197. Then on October 31st, 2003, with the Industrials closing at 9,801, this tool generated a primary-degree **buy signal** that led to **a four-year rally of 4,397 points, or 45 percent,** and to a new all-time nominal high on October 11th, 2007, at 14,198. Then the PTI generated a new long-term-trend sell signal on September 30th, 2008, just as the Great Recession's stock market crash started, when the Dow Jones 30 Industrial Average closed at 10,850. **We saw a 4,380 point – or 40 percent – drop after this sell signal was triggered in September of 2008, from 10,850 in the Industrials on September 30th, 2008, to 6,470 on March 6th, 2009.**

On May 31st, 2010, the PTI generated a new buy signal, and it remains on that buy signal now. Since that buy signal the Industrials have risen over 3,000 points, over 30 percent.

That is a pretty amazing predictive performance by a long-term indicator. **The point is that this indicator will be very useful in confirming when the coming Economic Ice Age**

has started. It is not the most precise indicator, as it does not change until several months after a new primary-trend turn has started. But once the signal changes we can be confident that the majority of the major new trend's price move is yet to come. **The next sell signal should identify when stocks have completed the Jaws of Death Grand-Supercycle-degree wave {III} top and the wave {IV} down Economic Ice Age is starting.**

In conclusion, we have a ballpark idea of when the coming **Economic Ice Age** will begin: sometime in 2014 or 2015 based on an extrapolation of the rising trend-line in the Jaws of Death pattern that prices have followed since March of 2009 (point (D) on the chart shown at the beginning of this chapter). **Confirmation that the Jaws of Death pattern is over and the Economic Ice Age has started will be received when the PTI generates a new sell signal**, which should occur several months after it has already started but in plenty of time to take advantage of a declining stock market with some investing strategies I will share with you later in this book. I want to keep repeating this: The purpose of this book is not to spread doom and gloom but to forewarn you of what the market is saying to us so you will have adequate time to prepare several financial strategies to survive and prosper during this lengthy and painful, but temporary, period of decline.

CHAPTER FOUR

Will There Be a World War during the Coming Economic Ice Age?

There will be considerable trouble during the coming Economic Ice Age. At this point the details of that trouble are largely speculative. An educated evaluation of the seeds of trouble that are currently gestating can give us insight into the future. There is one particular tribulation event that is more than pure speculation if history is any lesson. Repeatedly over the past three centuries – and longer if you want to go back to medieval and ancient times – economic calamity has led to large-scale war. That is a simple fact. Ergo, if wars have resulted from almost all previous economic collapses, then **there is a very high probability that world war will once again manifest from the coming Economic Ice Age.**

Further, history has demonstrated that the worse the economic downturn, the greater the war and resultant devastation to mankind. We are about to enter such a period of time. Let's take a look at the historic correlation of economic declines and the intensity of ensuing wars.

Let's start with the Revolutionary War, which resulted in major political change – the birth of America. It came after the Credit Crisis recession that hit Great Britain in 1772. According to Wikipedia (en.wikipedia.org):

Neal, James, Fordyce and Down was a London banking house which collapsed in June 1772, precipitating a major banking crisis which included the collapse of almost every private bank in Scotland, and a liquidity crisis in the two major banking centers of the world, London and Amsterdam. The bank had been speculating by shorting East India Company stock on a massive scale, and apparently using customer deposits to cover losses. The liquidity crisis spread to the next most important banking center in Europe, Amsterdam, where Clifford and Sons went bankrupt. The liquidity situation continued to be a problem into 1773. The crisis worsened relations between Britain and the Thirteen Colonies in America. Among other stresses, the East India Company, already in financial difficulties, was further weakened by the crisis, and in 1773 managed to persuade Parliament to pass the Tea Act, exempting it from the duty all other importers in the colonies had to pay. The unpopularity of this led to the Boston Tea Party at the end of the year.

And of course the Boston Tea Party triggered the Revolutionary War.

The War of 1812 between Great Britain and the United States was preceded by a three-year recession in the U.S. from 1807 to 1810. This recession was fed by the Embargo Act of 1807 during Thomas Jefferson's presidency, increasing tensions with Great Britain. It came at the same time trade restrictions were imposed by Great Britain, throwing shipping and commerce into a tailspin. The War of 1812 pulled the economy out of recession as war spending boosted commerce; however, as soon as the war ended, a six-year depression followed. This depression started with a financial panic during which bank notes lost their value due to wartime monetary overprinting. Real estate prices collapsed, foreclosures increased, and unemployment rose.

The Mexican-American War of 1846 to 1848 came on the heels of the economic depression of 1836 to 1843, during which business activity fell 34 percent. The cause of this first great depression of the nineteenth century was bank failures, the collapse of the cotton market, and asset deflation.

Just prior to the American Civil War from 1861 to 1865 was a recession known as the Panic of 1857, caused by the declining international economy and over-expansion of the U.S. domestic economy. Because of the interconnectedness of the world economy by the 1850s, the financial crisis that began in the autumn of 1857 was the first world-wide economic crisis. The tipping point that really set the Panic of 1857 in motion was the failure of Ohio Life Insurance and Trust Company.

The Spanish-American War of 1898 was preceded by the Panic of 1893 and an ensuing depression from 1895 to 1897 during which economic activity fell 25 percent.

World War I came in 1917 and lasted until 1918. It was preceded by the depression of 1913 to 1914 during which the economy fell 26 percent. The Federal Reserve Act and the creation of the Federal Reserve System were outcomes of this depression. It also marked the start of the Federal Income Tax system.

U.S. involvement in World War II, from 1941 to 1945, came on the heels of the Great Depression of the 1930s, which was kicked off by the stock market crash of 1929. The stock market crash and the ensuing economic collapse were global. U.S. gross domestic product (GDP) – the sum of all goods and services produced per year in our nation – fell 26 percent, which is an incredible slowdown when you consider a healthy economy sees GDP growth of 2 to 3 percent per year. After World War I, Germany's Weimar Republic experimented with printing huge amounts of money, which resulted in hyperinflation from 1921 to 1924, contributing to the start of the Great Depression and leading to the rise of the Third Reich and of course the start of WWII.

The Korean War arrived in 1950 and lasted until 1953. It was preceded by the recession of 1949 when GDP fell 1.7 percent.

The Vietnam War started in 1953 and lasted until 1975. This war was preceded by the recession of 1953 when GDP fell 2.6 percent, and was contemporaneous with several recessions – the recession of 1958 which saw GDP fall 3.7 percent, the recession of 1960-1961 when GDP fell 1.6 percent, the recession of 1969-1970 when GDP fell 0.6 percent, and the severe recession of 1973-1975 when GDP fell 3.2 percent.

There was a severe recession from 1980 to 1982 during which GDP fell 2.7 percent, which was followed by an escalation of the cold war between the United States and the Soviet Union. The result was an arms buildup unlike the world has ever seen, with unaccounted-for biological disease weapons such as Ebola pox, (a genetic combination of smallpox and the Ebola virus) and silos holding thousands of armed nuclear bombs capable of wiping out mankind.

The stock market crashes of 1987 and 1989 were followed by a recession from 1990 to 1991. That led to the Gulf War with Iraq from August of 1990 to March of 1991.

The recession from 2000 through 2002 led to the War on Terror and the Iraq War of 2003.

The Great Recession from 2007 through 2009 was contemporaneous with the War on Terror in Afghanistan, though no world war followed.

What we can conclude is that major wars do tend to break out within a few years of economic recessions and depressions, with a few exceptions. It makes sense when you think about it because economic declines increase tensions, increase scarcity, change political thought and economic policy, and lead to conflict. Wars cause nations to increase capital expenditures to ramp up military machinery, increase employment, and stimulate the economy. Wars often pull economies out of recessions and depressions. That does not mean that wars are planned purposefully to lead an economy out of recession, but rather it more likely means that that is the natural order of events.

The past tells us the probability is very high that the coming Economic Ice Age will result in a global war – likely within a few years of its start. The concern of course is that the Economic Ice Age will be severe and global, which means a resultant war could be global, threatening life as we know it. The last time there was a world war, we did not have the capability to wipe out mankind. This time we do. If World War III follows this economic calamity, it could place the world at the forefront of Armageddon. Is this inevitable? No. But the market is warning that trouble is dead ahead – trouble on a scale that perhaps has never been seen. It might take Divine intervention to stop the forces that are in motion. The Bible tells us that if Armageddon does occur, that is in fact what will happen – Divine intervention will stop it.

War can mean shortages; gold confiscation; price inflation for necessities such as food, oil, water, and medicines; and price depreciation for real estate, a dichotomy we have seen for the past few years as well. War means increased government spending for supplies, troops, military equipment, and manpower. Your perspective on war changes dramatically depending on whether it is fought on your soil or on foreign soil. Some of the unintended consequences of war we cannot prepare for include the drafting of children into the military like we saw during the Vietnam War and World War II. But steps can be taken to prepare for some of the consequences of war, and the strategies I present in coming chapters will be useful should war be in our future.

CHAPTER FIVE

The Sabotaging of the American Economy

At this point you might be asking, "How did we get in this Jaws of Death situation and what mistakes could have been prevented from a fundamental economics perspective?

Since 2000, our economy has been managed by the U.S. government differently than in the past. A *top-down* approach to economic stimulus has become the policy.

By top-down I mean that the government's policy has been to attempt to stimulate the real economy by flowing capital from a few large money-center banks such as J.P. Morgan, Goldman Sachs, and Citicorp down to households and small businesses – the guts of the economy – rather than using a *bottom-up* approach in which money flows from households up to small and large businesses and eventually toward large money-center banks and then to local, state, and federal governments in the form of tax receipts.

In a bottom-up approach to economic stimulation, marginal income tax rates are cut and/or income tax rebates are issued to households and small businesses. This approach recognizes that consumers (households) account for 70 percent of GDP and that small businesses account for 80 percent of all job growth. It empowers the middle class, offers opportunity for those in the lower socioeconomic class to elevate themselves through increased job opportunities and employer-funded training and education, and focuses prosperity on Main Street America. Increased spending fuels this economic engine, creating jobs, stimulating innovation, producing savings, and encouraging entrepreneurship and risk-taking. Capital investment increases and stuff is invented, produced, and sold. Revenues (the top line in the earnings equation) grow, corporate earnings increase, and **stock markets rise the right way, built on a broad-based demand for companies with growing price/earnings ratios (P/Es) in which revenues are the predominant reason for earnings growth rather than cost-cutting (a temporary fix for earnings).** In other words, earnings rise because of growth in sales, not contraction in spending.

The government is mainly in the business of national defense and infrastructure. It benefits from rising tax revenues, but that benefit should not be from an increase in marginal tax rates – from taking a larger piece of the pie – but from receiving a larger piece because of a much larger pie. The latter was the economics of Calvin Coolidge that kicked off the Roaring Twenties, of John Kennedy, of Ronald Reagan, and, to a lesser extent, of Bill Clinton, largely thanks in Clinton's case to the Contract with America bottom-up economic revolution of the 1994 Congress. **To start a bottom-up approach requires an initial large budget deficit increase as taxes are rebated and cut,** as if engaging a choke to start an engine; it appears to be an unproductive use of fuel, but shortly thereafter the engine is purring and producing more fuel than that initial start-up process required. **By the end of Bill Clinton's term we had achieved a budget surplus. America was prosperous. Main Street America did well. Households felt good.**

Things changed early in the 2000 millennium. Rather than accept a normal, mild correction – the natural cleansing process that free-market capitalism uses to prevent excesses that can lead to deep recessions and depressions, the decision was made to take a top-down approach to economic stimulus, attempt to minimize the economic correction, and keep the good times rolling. But **the game changed from real prosperity to artificial prosperity.**

We entered an age of economic oligarchy in our nation, and it started in a big way in the year 2000. The shift that took place equated the economy with Wall Street. But Wall Street is not the economy, and the economy is not Wall Street. Main Street (the little guy – households and small businesses) was no longer considered the key cog in economic growth. Wall Street, mega-money-center banks, and mega-corporations such as Exxon Mobil and Goldman Sachs were considered the relevant drivers of economic prosperity. If Main Street benefitted, great. But if it did not, so be it. Screw 'em! The goal was to make sure Wall Street financial firms made big money. Bigger was better. Industry consolidation was considered a good thing. Mom and Pop businesses were bought out so the mega-firm could control local markets. **If a few large firms could control commerce, the government could control all commerce by partnering with them.**

As this incestuous relationship grew throughout the decade, it became increasingly unclear whether it was government controlling the few large firms or the other way around. It hasn't mattered whether a Republican or a Democrat occupied the White House; the same top-down economic policy has been in force since 2000. The mantra has been, simply, if it is good for Goldman Sachs, it is good enough for everyone.

Obama was elected to change all this, but has done just the opposite. His administration and Congress have taken the master plan to new heights, to "central planning." And the question remains, is Obama leading or is Goldman Sachs, AIG, et al? Five trillion dollars have been spent to fix this economy over the past five years, but all that has been fixed are Goldman Sachs and the rest of the corporate oligarchy running this country. Targeted economic stimulus programs have been an abject failure, such as Cash for Clunkers, the token $10 a week average drop in income tax withholding requirements that the Obama administration trumpeted as a tax cut for 95 percent of all Americans in 2010, first-time home-buyers' tax credits, and the 2000-page multi-trillion-dollar national health insurance plan, Obamacare – whatever that contains – that people are still trying to figure out.

These targeted stimulus programs are nothing more than a propaganda scheme to try to hide the truth that fixing household finances is not on the agenda. Fixing the money-changers – the corporate Wall Street oligarchy – is the agenda. And it has been accomplished, at the price of devaluation of our currency, destruction of the job-generating machine, and escalation of our national budget deficit and national debt to incomprehensible levels. The central planners have achieved restoration of large Wall Street financial firms' health.

Exxon Mobil was taken care of in the middle of the 2000 decade, reaching record profits for any corporation in the history of the world while oil prices skyrocketed from $10 a barrel at the beginning of the decade to $147 a barrel in 2008. **The early 2000s saw the decision to indebt Main Street at the benefit of Wall Street and produce a fake prosperity for Main Street** and the "asset bubble" economy, during which housing values blew up like a balloon, then popped, but the debt that went along with them did not pop. It stuck to households like cow dung on boots.

Instead of allowing a mild recession and correction in the early 2000s, with Wall Street suffering along with the economy, it was decided to bypass that pain and replace real economic growth – bottom-up growth – with top-down, debt-induced, asset-bubble growth. Artificial growth. The President's Working Group on Financial Markets, also known as the Plunge Protection Team, or PPT (an oligarchy committee created by executive order number 12631 signed on March 18th, 1988, in response to the 1987 stock market crash), consisting of the Secretary of the Treasury, the Chairperson of the Federal Reserve, the Chairperson of the Securities and Exchange Commission, the Chairperson of the Commodities Futures Trading Commission, and their surrogates – the major Wall Street firms – were on the job pushing stock markets higher from 2003 through 2007. Key members of the PPT including the Secretary of the Treasury, the Chairperson of the Fed, and the large Wall Street financial firms did their part by quadrupling the money supply over the first decade of the 2000s. The approach was simple: either the PPT would buy stock futures indices directly or purchase fixed-income securities from Wall Street, who would take the cash and buy stock futures indices or other commodities. The inevitable result of all this was the stock market crash of 2007 into 2009.

The Republicans were thrown out by Main Street America in the election of 2008 with the expectation that the Democrats would get back to using a bottom-up approach to economic policy. It was hoped money would be placed into the hands of Main Street – households and small businesses – in a manner other than debt from Wall Street or debt from banks that acted as tentacles for Wall Street. Those banks were lending money then selling the debt to Wall Street, which restructured that debt into toxic assets (such as collateralized mortgage-obligation securities, subprime and prime mortgage-backed securities, and asset-backed consumer-loan securities) that would ultimately be bought by everyone from individuals via their 401(k)s to pension funds, mutual funds, local governments, hedge funds, and ultimately large Wall Street firms.

Some of those Wall Street firms were allowed to fail, such as Lehman Brothers, or forced into shotgun marriages such as that between Merrill Lynch and Bank of America. Others were bailed out at massive taxpayer expense, such as AIG. Others quietly prospered, benefitted, and had a lot to say about how the entire economic crisis was handled, such as survivors Goldman Sachs, J.P. Morgan, and Citicorp. Right now the Federal Reserve is buying those toxic assets from Wall Street in exchange for freshly printed dollars through a Fed stimulus program known as quantitative easing – the fourth round (QE4). This is one sweet deal for Wall Street.

If you watch CNBC, you really get the feeling that all that matters in today's economy are the big-boy firms. Goldman this, Citicorp that. Very little attention to Mom and Pop other than encouraging them to jump back in with their decimated account balances and buy, buy, buy. Main Street is irrelevant to government, Wall Street, and the financial media.

The artificial rally from March of 2009 through the writing of this book is very similar to the artificial rally from March of 2003 through 2007. Almost the entire rally over that four-year timespan occurred on a fraction of days of huge price gains. The same thing occurred again during the rally from March of 2009 to 2010. **Over a forty-three-week period, 80 percent of the price gains of that rally occurred on thirty Mondays.** What this tells us is that this might not have been a broad-based rally; rather it showed the signs and symptoms of a sporadic, deep-pockets intervention. **If I am correct, and a myriad of technical charts and indicators I follow suggest I am, another massive stock market decline is coming. Folks inclined to trust the central planners might be behaving as sheep, mindlessly placing all their eggs in the Wall Street** basket without evidence of sound fundamental economic growth and prosperity at the household and small-business level. This is a lot like playing craps at a casino table. It's a dangerous economic time for investors regardless of whether the plunge starts sooner or later.

Let's look at those fundamentals:

The **federal deficit** could approach 1.2 trillion dollars in 2013, 8 percent of GDP. (Remember, our budget was balanced back in 2000!) Do you understand the pressure this will put on the dollar and on interest rates? This is forcing the Federal Reserve to buy dollars and U.S. Treasury securities in the open market to support the dollar's price *and* keep short- and long-term interest rates low. But it cannot do both. Buying securities requires spending (selling) dollars. **This strategy means the dollar eventually has to tank or interest rates eventually have to rise to high heaven. In either case, real economic growth will suffer and the U.S. standard of living will decline.** In my opinion, it is the dollar that will be sacrificed, not Treasuries (interest rates). A ton of the $1.0 trillion annual U.S. deficits each year from 2010 through 2012 went to Wall Street mega-firm bailouts, not to Main Street America. Why? Because they have the power. Because we are being governed under economic oligarchy, not economic democracy.

We are borrowing to pay the interest on our national debt. The U.S. is bringing in tax revenues equal to only 74 percent of what it is spending annually. The solution should be to increase the economic pie on which taxes are assessed. However, the trend is to increase taxes on the same size pie: "Tax the rich!" *Rich* is defined as the small businessman who takes huge risks, works 100 hours a week, provides jobs to a dozen or so people, and manages to make $250,000 a year for himself, which he will use to put his four kids through college at schools that charge $40,000 per year in tuition (total cost for college for those kids: $640,000, assuming tuition costs do not rise).

There were 1.12 million bankruptcy filings in the U.S. in 2008. There were 1.43 million bankruptcy filings in 2009. In 2010 there were 1.59 million bankruptcy filings. In 2011 there were 1.41 million bankruptcy filings. In 2012 there were 1.25 million bankruptcy filings added to the pile. Not many folks file for bankruptcy twice in five years, which means these accumulating numbers total 6.8 million over the past five years. There are 79.3 million families in America. Think about that ratio. And this is before the coming Economic Ice Age hits. The point is that we are heading into this Economic Ice Age from a position of weakness.

Jobs. You ready for these numbers? The Bureau of Labor Statistics, a division of the U.S. Labor Department, reported January 8th, 2013, that by their count, **22.7 million people, or 14.5 percent of the labor force, were either unemployed or involuntarily stuck with part-time jobs in December of 2012 when they really wanted full-time work.** The unemployment rate they reported was 7.8 percent, but if you include unemployed people who wanted work but had not searched for work in the past four weeks for various reasons, the unemployment rate was 9.5 percent. By comparison, the unemployment rate was 5.0 percent in December of 2007.

The Labor Department reported that the economy gained 155,000 non-farm payroll jobs in December of 2012. If you consider we need to generate 150,000 new jobs each month to accommodate new entrants into the labor force, it means December's employment change barely met what was necessary to break even and fell woefully short of enough jobs to recover those that have been lost over the past five years. How in the world is this economy going to create 22.7 million jobs any time soon, or even one million jobs for that matter, with the central-planner, top-down policies being followed? Answer: it can't and it won't. **This also tells us that we will be entering the coming Economic Ice Age from a position of weakness.**

More on the December jobs data: The average workweek came in at 34.5 hours, near record lows. The Labor Department defines long-term unemployment as twenty-seven weeks. 4.8 million good folks had been unemployed at least that long.

These statistics do not even begin to address quality of jobs, but all you need to know about that is that 7.9 million Americans wanted full-time work in December but had to settle involuntarily for part-time work.

In summary, as far as jobs go, fewer people are working, more folks are dropping out of the labor pool, and those who are working are working fewer hours now than was the case a decade ago.

Wow, this new top-down economic policy that started under Bush in the early 2000s and has been taken to new heights by the Obama administration, while both Republican and Democrat Congresspersons have sat by applauding, has really worked, hasn't it? Like the general said to his surviving troops, "It depends on your point of view."

Let's examine the success of this new top-down economic policy being run by our new form of government, oligarchy:

Goldman Sachs earned $7.38 billion net income in 2012, with J.P. Morgan earning a record $21.5 billion net income in 2012, and Citicorp earning $7.5 billion in 2012. And even Bank of America is doing fine, thank you ma'am, at over $4.2 billion for 2012. Not to worry, Exxon Mobil made over $44 billion in 2012. So the central planners' policies have in fact worked for the big boys. All is well with the world.

Main Street America? They are irrelevant. But isn't the stock market rallying? Isn't that helping Main Street America get back on its feet? No. Only one-third of all Americans own over $10,000 in stocks, and 82 percent of all publically traded directly owned stocks are owned by 5 percent of the population, according to an "Inside Wealth" report by CNBC on February 1st, 2013, which cited data from the Economic Policy Institute. Top-down economic policy might have helped the stock market over the past few years, but it is not helping Main Street America.

Speaking of the stock market, how did the stock market do with the top-down policy from 2000 through 2012? The Industrials rose a total of 13.9 percent over that twelve-year span, about 1.1 percent per year on average (less than 1.0 percent if you compound returns). The S&P 500 lost 43 points over the past twelve years. **The S&P 500 has not gained anything in twelve years!** Cash vastly outperformed both the S&P 500 and the Industrials. The NASDAQ Composite remains down a huge 25.8 percent. Cash beat the tar out of technology stocks. And the money supply increased in size by five times over the past twelve years to achieve this, with the dollar losing half its trade-weighted value. At first blush, if you are a central planner – a member of the oligarchy running this nation – you might be disturbed by these figures; but probably no more than you are by the housing, unemployment, and bankruptcy numbers. Why? Because you still have power and your companies are still making big money. The bonuses are flowing. It's okay.

What we have witnessed over the past decade, and continue to witness, is nothing more than the sabotage of the American economy. We elected three administrations to conduct this policy. The American household drank the Kool-

Aid. They believed the smooth-talking rhetoric. They ceded their power to an oligarchy – rule by a few powerful individuals. Main Street America needs to yank that power back and return this great nation to the democracy our founding fathers established, by holding our representatives and our out-of-control executive branch accountable for their oversight and policy mistakes.

At the next congressional elections, any politician who had anything to do with this economic mess should be tossed out on his or her pampered derriere and replaced with a populist candidate who believes in bottom-up capitalism, low marginal tax rates, and aggressive policies to kick-start the American household, small businesses, and small banks. The next election might be our last chance, if several ominous bearish prediction models such as the Jaws of Death are accurate in their forecasts that stock markets world-wide will begin a decade-long plunge starting sometime in 2014 or 2015.

We the people should direct Congress to change the entire economic approach from top-down to bottom-up. The economy is in a death spiral, and that needs to be stopped and reversed. To do so at this point, because so much time and money has been wasted and so much damage has occurred over the past twelve years, drastic action is necessary.

The solution: There needs to be a massive income tax rebate, along the lines of two years of income taxes, returned to each and every household immediately, with a minimum payment of $50,000. It should be required that half of that be used for debt repayment. The benefit would be to clean up household balance sheets, improving household credit ratings, keeping folks in their homes, and providing bridge financing without debt burden for the unemployed to start businesses or retrain themselves through education. This would trickle up benefits to small and large businesses, as folks would have more money to start spending, stimulating the economy. Further, this income tax rebate would substantially improve the balance sheets of small banks by metamorphosing delinquent loans into current status, and by repaying charged-off loans. This would benefit banks by increasing capital levels, reducing loan balances, increasing lending capacity via improved loan-to-deposit and loan-to-capital ratios, and improving liquidity, all without the need for government intervention.

As the economy revived itself through this bottom-up process, corporations' price/earnings ratios would improve, with improvement coming from the top line rather than cost cuts, which in turn would boost stock prices fundamentally – not artificially, resulting in more grassroots interest in purchasing market investments. Money would trickle up to large Wall Street investment banking firms, where capital would be available for productive investment. The cost of such a program would be $5 trillion, but the Treasury Department could raise that money quickly by issuing securities to the Fed in exchange for cash. Then as profits rose from individual and corporate earnings, tax revenues would also rise for local, state, and federal governments as the total economic pie grew. This program would generate enough tax revenues over time to reduce deficits and repay newly issued U.S. Treasury securities without the need to raise marginal tax rates.

As a simultaneous side stimulus program, **real estate taxes should be abolished and replaced with consumption taxes.** This removes a rapidly growing onerous property confiscation tax, which is unconstitutional anyway, and replaces it with a tax that is born by those who can more easily afford it – buyers of goods and services. Senior citizens and unemployed folks are getting murdered by property taxes.

Finally, a third piece of this bottom-up solution is to reduce marginal income tax rates to an eventual 10 percent flat tax, period. Simple and affordable.

This program makes far too much sense to actually be adopted, and to be honest it looks as if we are too far gone to effect this change. The present oligarchy is like a runaway freight train rushing downhill. There just might be too much momentum to stop it. Perhaps if there were some sort of grassroots "Contract with America" revival in time for the next congressional elections we might have half a chance. But so far there is very little noise out there suggesting anything of the sort.

To revive the real estate market, there needs to be an initial kick-start of the engine – a lowering of down payment requirements. While at first this might sound risky – risky for lenders – again, they would have plenty of capital and plenty of money to lend if the above tax policies were enacted. In the past, individuals and businesses could purchase real estate with as little as 5 or 10 percent down. But because of the deflationary spiral in real estate values, banks became more conservative and increased required down payments to 20 to 30 percent for all buyers, whether high income / high net worth or not.

The primary economic problem for households and small businesses is coming up with cash in an environment in which real estate values have not risen and have in fact declined 10 to 50 percent, fixed-income yields are at historic lows, tax burdens from state and local income tax assessments have increased, local property assessments have gone up, and federal entitlement and income taxes are higher. How does a household or small business build the cash necessary to afford a 20 to 30 percent down payment on real estate when jobs are being lost, salaries are being cut, and quality high-paying jobs are being replaced with lower paying jobs or a couple of part-time near-minimum-wage jobs? If the government wants to do something productive, it should set up a national insurance program for the difference between a 5 percent down payment and the 20 percent that lending institutions now want. If a buyer qualifies for the monthly payments they should automatically be accepted by this down payment insurance program. High down payment requirements have been a self-fulfilling prophecy, virtually eliminating demand and driving property values down. With the increased demand for properties that would result from this down payment insurance program, the real estate market would turn around fast and be a big boost to the economy. Construction would increase, as would jobs and revenues for small and large businesses that supply the construction industry.

Europe's sovereign debt woes continue, and calls for austerity impact its economies negatively (taking money out of the economy is recessionary). Europe is between a rock and a hard place. If it does not cut government expenditures, sovereign debt overload will crush European countries. Right now Spain, Portugal, Greece, and Italy are essentially bankrupt. But if they cut spending they will contract their economies, risking depression. With the global interdependence between economies, if one nation goes down, all nations could. Europe's problems will undoubtedly spill over to the United States.

One out of every four dollars spent in the U.S. is spent on health care, and that ratio is only going to get worse as baby boomers age. This is a non-productive national expenditure that does not produce new GDP. If a person becomes ill, their illness becomes a drain on the economy, not a stimulant. Is it possible that there is too much unnecessary testing going on? Are there too many drugs being prescribed? Are there too many unnecessary examinations with medical professionals, raising the cost of health care to unsustainable levels? Is there too much concern with early detection; too much reliance on the medical profession and not enough use of preventive and homeopathic treatments that are far less expensive such as herbs, vitamins, exercise, and healthy diets? Is it too important that for-profit hospitals keep their censuses up, have all rooms occupied and all machines running, regardless of the necessity for patient health care? Look at the money being spent on television ads that use fear to motivate you to go for testing and treatment. And all the legal disclaimers in drug commercials warning about serious side effects which of course would require another trip back to the hospital. Nutty, isn't it?

Our educational system is a mess. Increased school taxes have led to more dollars spent on unnecessary items (for example, the lunacy of Astroturf fields and theatre stages that rival some on Broadway); teachers unions turning teachers into assignors and judges; provoked kids; angry young adults; poor math and English skills; elitist private elementary, middle, and high schools; elitist universities to which it is nearly impossible to gain entry; overemphasis on entrance exam test scores for college admission; and overemphasis on memorizing useless facts inside the box at the expense of creative outside-the-box thinking. Steve Jobs and Bill Gates dropped out of college because their creativity was stifled. There is too much labeling of students who learn differently as "special needs" – a damaging stigma that leaves children feeling rejected, odd, unaccepted. Pressure, pressure, pressure on kids to the point that they are angry at society by the time they get out of high school. Government-mandated rules, regulations, standards – this is why the home-school movement is growing rapidly in America and why it is so successful and a whole lot cheaper for taxpayers.

After the Fiscal Cliff resolution on January 1st, 2013, we now have the highest tax rates on top earners since 1979. Including federal, state, local, and entitlement taxes, the rate is as high as 50 percent in the U.S. This penalizes success and is a disincentive to take business chances, hire people, and build a larger tax pie. Class warfare is a huge deterrent to economic growth and a key contributor to the coming Economic Ice Age.

Low-tax nations like Hong Kong and Singapore have faster economic growth rates than high-tax nations such as European nations and the United States that aim to punish success to pay for more entitlements for those looking to government for provision, as if government is Dear Granddad in the sky. The more money flowing to Washington D.C., the more inefficiency and waste of money occurs.

President Kennedy gave perhaps the most famous inaugural address ever, uttering the words "Ask not what your country can do for you – ask what you can do for you country." Think about those words. The escalation of entitlements in the U.S. and Europe, to many who are not in serious need, is bankrupting economies and asking too much of our countries. When folks look to government for solutions to most or all of their problems, and government acquiesces, motivated to obtain control over the citizenry and get their votes, you get sovereign bankruptcy and the death of free-market capitalism. Simple free-market capitalism is our best bet for a bigger pie for all to share, and government entitlement obsession is a surefire bet for a shrinking pie and a situation in which all lose and the Economic Ice Age comes like a thief in the night.

In the absence of the necessary fix, the technical picture suggests that a worst-case scenario is likely. A fix will not come soon. The bear market will continue and worsen. **That is why I dedicate the next five chapters to how you personally can prepare to survive and prosper during the coming Economic Ice Age.**

A little history from ancient Greece: A policy of allowing a few powerful individuals – in our case Wall Street mega-banking firms – to drive government economic policy (which is what we see going on now; almost every Treasury Secretary comes from either the New York Fed or a New York money-center bank) is called an oligarchy, not a democracy – not even a republic. *Oligarchy* means "rule by a few" in Greek. **Almost the entire stimulus plan took the form of cash handouts to a few large financial corporations. Nothing of any substance has been provided to the masses – to the people who elect representatives, who elect our government.** Somehow the central planners are heeding the wishes of the likes of Goldman Sachs and friends, with ill-regard for moms and pops on Main Street America. Oligarchy was the politics of ancient Greece from 800 to 650 B.C. **Resentment of aristocratic power followed and led to dictatorship. The age of the tyrants followed oligarchy in Greece from 650 to 500 BC.** The central planner group running the U.S. has chosen a parallel policy and decision-making road, a dangerous path that could have consequences in the U.S. similar to those it had in ancient Greece.

In summary, a ton of central-planner money has gone into a few large Wall Street firms, with very little landing in the hands of consumers or small businesses, many of which are small, family-owned enterprises. **The central planners have essentially said, "Hey, if you want money, play ball with the large banks and the few large firms we gave your money to. Borrow more if you can or take your substantially lower account balances and buy stocks from the few big firms we are interested in helping. And good luck."** Households are not getting direct help from the powers with the means to give it. Job losses continue, salary increases are non-existent, debts are overwhelming and below collateral values, and there is not much hope on the horizon that incomes will increase. Stocks generally rise about 70 percent of the time, but what is critical is where prices land. Bear markets and declines can wipe out gains in far less time than it takes to generate them. We saw that happen in the past decade time and time again, and I believe it's going to happen again this decade, starting as soon as 2014 or 2015.

CHAPTER SIX

Strategy One: Build Cash and Reduce Debts

Cash is king in economic depressions. Cash is the best medium of exchange. It is lightweight, easy to carry, durable, easy to store, and widely accepted for buying and selling. Cash can be more broadly defined as money or currency. It is money in the bank, in a comparable money-market fund, in your wallet, under your mattress, or in a fire-proof safe. When prices decline in an economic depression, the purchasing power of cash increases. Although there is minimal or no return on cash per se, if stock prices are dropping, bond prices are falling, and/or real estate values are declining, the purchasing power of cash increases. Having cash in an economic collapse provides you with opportunity. It gives you peace of mind in the face of a chaotic and frightening world.

In the coming economic collapse, it is going to be hard to come up with cash. Jobs will be lost, wages will decline, investment returns will drop, asset values will decline, buyers of hard assets such as houses will be absent, and taxes will increase to fund government. You need to pay the mortgage and buy groceries and necessities. You need cash sitting somewhere safe and easy to access to weather the Economic Ice Age.

If you place cash in a bank account or money-market account at a brokerage firm, you must pay attention to the financial strength of those financial institutions. Limit balances in financial institutions to the maximum amount insured by the Federal Deposit Insurance Corporation (FDIC). What makes this tough is the FDIC insurance limit might decline as the economy worsens. If the FDIC fund collapses, it might drop insurance from $250,000 to $100,000 or to $50,000 per account holder. If the bank you have your money in is closed down, you might have to wait months, maybe years for the FDIC to return it to you. During the 2007 to 2009 recession, major long-time investment banks such as Lehman Brothers collapsed very fast with little warning. We will not be able to rely on the accuracy of financial institutions' financial statements because economic destruction can happen to a large money-center bank before financial statements are updated after the next quarterly reporting period. You cannot assume that a financial institution is safe just because its financial statement for the prior quarter is strong.

Therefore, cash should be spread around to many different FDIC-insured financial institutions to defend yourself against the sudden surprise collapse of any one particular institution. A stricter regulatory requirement for minimum capital levels at a bank can turn a going concern into a failed institution without any changes to its balance sheet. **And there is risk to your money from legislation.** Once the economy tanks, there is a very good chance that the government will increase bank capital requirements and start classifying historically good loans as bad loans, forcing good banking institutions into closure overnight and putting your money at risk.

It is important to hold lots of cash in your home in a hidden, fireproof safe or vault. As this calamity deepens, there will be risks involved in accessing gasoline, making it harder to get to the bank to get your money. Companies that run software for ATMs could collapse; merchant credit card processing companies could fold up, shutting down small businesses; cash could become very difficult to access even from your bank. There could be runs on banks like back in the 1930s. So you should safely hide a lot of cash on your property.

Which currency should you hold? Many different currencies? One in particular? I answer this question this way: Pick the currency of a nation that you believe will still be standing during and after the coming world war. Pick the currency of a nation that has a strong military and a fairly stable political structure. If you want to diversify, have some currency from a second nation or a third. Maybe the U.S. dollar is your first choice. It would be mine. Maybe some euros would be good. Maybe some Swiss francs. Think about the U.S. Civil War in the 1860s. Confederate currency was good only until the Civil War ended. Then it was worthless.

Debt is death in an economic depression. The good book tells us the debtor is the slave of the creditor. While building up cash you should simultaneously pay off debt. Start with your highest-interest-rate, lowest-balance credit cards, then pay off the next-highest-interest-rate, lowest-balance debt, and so on. While it is probably impossible for everyone to pay off all their debts before this Economic Ice Age starts, get rid of any loan that requires renewal. You cannot count on the bank renewing the loan upon term expiration. If you must have debt, it would be great if you can end up with only a low-interest-rate mortgage.

Beware of the right of *set-off*. Many banks hide in the fine print of loan agreements that they have the right to seize your money from your deposit account with them for various reasons. One is probably if you are late making payments. Another might be if the term expires and they choose not to renew your unpaid loan or line of credit. Or they might even have an "at will" clause that allows them to accelerate your loan payments should your financial position change adversely, such as they get wind that you lost your job or have more debt than when you first got the loan. To protect yourself from unwanted seizure of your cash, you might want to hold your largest cash balances in banks you do not borrow from, and keep minimal cash in banks you do borrow from.

The more debt you pay off, the more cash you will save every month to further pay down other debt and build cash balances. It is a process – a lengthy one. But the sooner you start, the better.

We cannot count on the government preventing foreclosures on delinquent mortgages. There were 750,000 foreclosures in 2012. Your mortgage should be the first payment you make every month, on time, to be sure you maintain shelter. If you are unable to pay off all your debt before the Economic Ice Age hits and shuts down all your income, and something has to go delinquent, let it be something unsecured such as a credit card. The caveat is that once you are delinquent on credit cards, your credit rating goes down the crapper. The best situation is to pay off all debts, have a low-interest-rate mortgage only if you must have some debt, and pay that mortgage payment on time.

In bad economic times, banks are not your friends. They will be getting the snot kicked out of them by federal bank regulators and will be forced to shut down lending or raise standards such that even credit-worthy individuals and loyal customers will be hard-pressed to get a loan. Federal examiners and Congress will get blamed as banks fail, so they will react by doing exactly the opposite of what is best for the economy – they will shut down lending. Why? They will do so to protect their derrieres, afraid that taxpayers will blame them for not preventing banks from making bad loans. We saw this during the 1990 to 1991 recession, when it essentially cost George Herbert Bush a second term as president. It happened again during the 2000 to 2002 recession, and again during the 2007 to 2009 recession.

You can see that the contraction in the economy will be self-perpetuating. Normally economies grow as people borrow and invest in property, business ventures, and investments. But banks will be forced to shut the spigot at the worst possible time. Politicians will be so worried about looking tough to their voter/taxpayer base that once the public hears banks are failing, Congress will pass restrictions on banks that essentially shut down the lending function and kill the economy after it is already sick. Be ready for this. There is an old adage that goes: "Bank regulators are the ones who enter the battlefield after it is over and shoot the wounded."

What about the risk that sovereign nations will simply print money to make up for shrinking GDPs? Won't that weaken the value of currencies? Yes and no. Yes, the nation that prints the most will have a weaker-valued currency than other nations; however, the economy and the money supply will be shrinking so fast that the cash that is printed will likely only make up a portion of the money supply. Due to the shutdown of lending, the money supply will decline from a reverse-multiplier, velocity-of-money event. For all practical purposes you will need cash to conduct transactions regardless of how much is being printed. The cost of necessities such as oil, water, food, and medicine could rise as inflation due to the printing of money rises. We have seen this dichotomy over the past several years from the quantitative-easing printing of trillions of U.S. dollars by the Federal Reserve. The effect has been hyperinflation in necessities (which has gone largely unreported in official Consumer Price Index (CPI) statistics), but depreciation in the value of real estate. The value of stocks, bonds, and real estate will decline in spite of hyperinflationary printing of U.S. dollars because of a lack of confidence in the future (stocks), weakening credit ratings and higher monetary inflation (bonds), and a lack of lender-acceptable buyers (real estate).

The Federal Reserve will continue to inject cash into the economy the wrong way, to the wrong people. There have been four quantitative-easing programs since 2008, and all they have done is print cash and place it in the hands of a few huge, powerful, money-center banks in New York City. It has not trickled down to households or small businesses, and has failed to revive the economy. This top-down approach to economic stimulation has failed. And that is what they will do again. Cash is king in an economic depression. Start saving now.

Strategy Two: Gold, Silver, and Mining Stocks

It could be very important to own some gold and silver for several reasons. First, these precious metals are an inflation hedge should the Fed print too many dollars. Gold and silver should keep pace, rising in value as the total volume of dollars – the total money supply – rises, which I believe will occur during the coming Economic Ice Age. Printing lots of cash is a key step the Fed will take to inject liquidity into Wall Street by exchanging freshly printed dollars for securities – probably poor-credit-worthy securities held by the large mega-center banks or securities at risk of a deteriorating credit rating.

If you hold precious metals and forget about them, you should have an asset that increases in value as the economy gets flushed down the john. Initially you can choose to own gold in the form of an exchange-traded fund (ETF) for convenience, such as GLD for gold, or for silver, SLV. However, as the Economic Ice Age deepens, there is increasing risk that the custodian of the physical metal that backs up the ETF will become bankrupt, or that government confiscation laws will be enacted that force the custodian to hand over the precious metal to the government, and you will be left with something else – such as dollars, or nothing.

U.S. government confiscation of gold occurred back in the 1930s. During the Great Depression, President Franklin Roosevelt and Congress passed a confiscation law requiring gold to be handed in to the government (Executive Order # 6102). They gave everyone about one month (from April 3rd, 1933, to May 1st, 1933) to return all gold coins, gold bullion, and gold certificates to the Federal Reserve in exchange for $20.67 per ounce (as this book is being written, gold is worth $1,250 per ounce). Failure to do this was punishable by a $10,000 fine (which is equivalent to over $150,000 today) and/or up to ten years in prison. Many people who had gold did not return it to the U.S. government but hid it in safe deposit boxes in Swiss or other foreign banks. Hitler did the same thing during World War II, confiscating gold from the German people. So at some point early in the Economic Ice Age you will want to abandon ETFs, or at least minimize their percentage of your portfolio, and opt to hold physical gold and silver so you can retain more control and have more options should another confiscation occur.

A second reason to hold gold and silver is that if a new currency replaces the U.S. dollar, these precious metals will provide you with a means of exchange that will retain its value relative to the new currency. If fiat paper currency is replaced by new fiat paper currency, gold and silver will be worth just as much in proportion to the new currency as to the old. How could our currency be replaced by a new one? If the massive amount of unfunded liabilities ($122 trillion) and the actual debt of the United States ($16.5 trillion) become so large that it is virtually impossible to repay them, exchanging dollars for a new currency – "Americas," for example – is a step the government would likely take. A thousand or a hundred thousand dollars would be worth one "America" unit of exchange. It is a way for the U.S. (or any other nation for that matter) to repudiate, or cancel, its debts. Voilà, debt is gone. If you are holding dollars when this happens, you get screwed. But if you are holding gold or silver, it will maintain its value in the new currency.

Possessing precious metals will protect you from future government repudiation of its debts. Truthfully, it will be impossible for the U.S. government to pay off its debts given its tendency to raise taxes, redistribute income, increase entitlements, increase pork-barrel spending, increase the size of government and the number of government employees, and mandate entitlement expenses from small businesses such as with Obamacare. These actions fail to increase the size of the total economy that income taxes can be assessed against, so tax collections fall woefully short in raising the money necessary to meaningfully pay down or pay off the national debt. Even if the government raised income taxes to 100 percent on every man, woman, child, and business, it would not even come close to paying off the national debt. That means debt repudiation is in our future, maybe once the Economic Ice Age is so deep that drastic steps are all that are left.

A third reason to hold gold and silver is as a means of exchange – to be used as a currency to buy stuff, especially necessities. For this purpose, I favor owning coins – small denomination coins mostly, because you won't be able to get change from a merchant if you hand him a brick of gold to buy a bag of groceries. Silver dimes, quarters, gold dollars – the smaller the better. The more the better. Hold them in a fireproof safe or vault, hidden from discovery.

A fourth purpose in holding gold and silver, and especially gold, is as a geopolitical safe haven. Whenever crises arise, the value of gold rises. The crisis could be war, widespread natural disasters, global contagion, climate change, or political revolution such as was seen in Russia and Germany in the early 1900s. Gold does well during times of great fear. The coming Economic Ice Age will birth great fear.

Gold has been higher in value against the U.S. dollar for the last twelve years in a row. You cannot print gold. It is up in value against all other currencies over the past ten years. When people start to see major financial corporations dissolve as the Economic Ice Age deepens, demand for gold and silver will skyrocket. When confidence in the economic system fails, gold and silver will be coveted. That is what motivated Roosevelt to confiscate gold in 1933; people were hoarding it.

We are in a bad spot right now. Look at these numbers: Our federal budget deficit is $1.07 trillion per year, and that is after collecting federal tax revenues of $2.4 trillion – 15.5 percent of GDP. GDP is $15.5 trillion – less than the federal debt which is $16.5 trillion. Total debt, including federal, state, and local government; business; and individual debt, is a whopping $58 trillion. The national debt per taxpayer is $145,000. Personal debt per citizen in the U.S. is $52,192. That means that when a baby is born, it is already in debt by over $50,000. The annual interest on all the personal and government debt in the U.S. is $3.3 trillion – about 20 percent of GDP. How is all this debt ever going to get paid back? It is not. A day of reckoning is coming.

Now consider our government's unfunded liabilities, which are not even on the books yet as debt. The Social Security obligation is $16.1 trillion. The Prescription Drug liability is $21.3 trillion. The Medicare liability is an incredible $84.8 trillion. The total of just those three entitlement commitments is an astronomical $122 trillion. That works out to over $1.0 million per taxpayer.[1] Are you kidding? Where is that money going to come from? Some new scheme that will change everything is the only answer. Gold as a safe haven? You bet.

How did gold and silver perform during the last three stock market plunges? From July 5th to August 9th, 2011, the Dow Industrials had a mini-crash, falling 2,116 points, or 16.6 percent. During that crash, gold rose 270 points, or 17.8 percent, and silver rose 5.24 points, or 14.8 percent. Gold and silver prospered as stocks plunged. From October 9th, 2007, through March 6th, 2009, the Dow Industrials fell 7,695 points, or 54.3 percent. During that same precise time period, gold rose 200 points, or 27.2 percent, and silver rose 0.25 points, or 1.9 percent; gold prospered and silver held its own. During the previous stock market crash, from January 14th, 2000, through October 10th, 2002, the Industrials plunged 4,525 points, or 38.6 percent. However, gold rose 34.8 points, or 12.2 percent, and silver fell 0.74 points, losing 14.5 percent; gold prospered and silver lost substantially less value than the Industrials' stocks did.

A fifth reason to hold gold and silver is because more and more we are seeing them used as industrial products – in electronics, computers, medicine, aerospace, and jewelry. Look at the attributes of gold: it conducts electricity, does not tarnish, is malleable, can be made into wire, can be pressed into thin sheets, alloys with many other metals, can be liquefied and cast into intricate shapes, and has a beautiful color and a brilliant luster (of course this is part of its appeal for use in jewelry). The most important industrial use of gold is in the manufacture of electronics. Solid-state electronic devices use very low voltages and currents that are easily interrupted by corrosion or tarnish at contact points. Gold is the highly efficient conductor that can carry these tiny currents and remain free of corrosion. Electronic components made with gold are highly reliable. Gold is used in connectors, switch and relay contacts, soldered joints, connecting wires, and connection strips. A small amount of gold is used in almost every sophisticated electronic device including cell phones, calculators, personal digital assistants, and global positioning system units. Most large electronic appliances such as television sets also contain gold. What this means is that gold is being used up on a grand scale, and gold is not a limitless resource. Over time this can only add to gold's value.[2]

And of course gold is used in computers. The rapid and accurate transmission of digital information within a computer and from one component to another requires an efficient and reliable conductor. Gold meets these requirements better than any other metal. The importance of high-quality and reliable performance justifies the high cost. Edge connectors used to mount microprocessor and memory chips on motherboards contain gold, as do plug-and-socket connectors used to attach cables. The gold in these components is generally electroplated onto other metals and alloyed with small amounts of nickel or cobalt to increase durability.[2]

Gold is also used in the medical and aerospace industries. It is used in certain drugs to treat conditions including rheumatoid arthritis, in radiology treatments, and in electronic equipment used for life support. In the aerospace industry it is used as a mechanical lubricant, in electronic circuitry, and to reflect infrared radiation and keep a spacecraft's temperature stable.[2]

Mining stocks are a unique hybrid of investing in precious metals and an operating company. The stock market is likely to plunge during the Economic Ice Age, but precious metals are likely to rally. When you invest in gold and silver you are investing in precious metals that are already above ground; when you invest in mining stocks you are investing in what is still underground. So there is more risk in holding mining stocks such as GDX than in holding the precious metals themselves. There is operating risk in mining stocks in as far as how the mining company obtains working capital to dig, regulatory restrictions, etc. For the coming Economic Ice Age I favor holding gold and silver over holding mining stocks.

Mining stocks, as measured by the New York Stock Exchange's Arca Gold BUGS Index, or HUI, performed more unpredictably during the three stock market plunges cited above. During the

July 2011 to August 2011 stock market plunge, mining stocks rose 4 percent. During the 2007 through 2009 stock market plunge, mining stocks fell 28.4 percent – about half the loss that the Dow Industrials experienced. During the 2000 to 2003 stock market collapse, mining stocks rose 60 percent while stocks fell 38 percent.

1.   U.S. Debt Clock.org
2.   "The many uses of Gold," Herbert King, www.geology.com

How Do I Buy Physical Gold and Silver?

Okay, so you have decided you want your total portfolio to have somewhere between 10 and 20 percent invested in physical gold and silver precious metals. Let's now explore the process of building this segment of your portfolio; what are you buying exactly, and how will you go about doing this? The assumption is that you have never bought physical gold or silver as an investment before. Let's begin.

The first step is to **understand the kind of gold and silver you are going to buy.** There is gold, and then again there is gold. Same with silver. Let's start with gold. **There are three types of gold you can buy: 1) jewelry, 2) numismatic, or 3) bullion.** You do not want to invest in jewelry. There are issues as far as receiving full value for the gold and illiquidity (meaning it is harder to find a ready marketplace – harder to find buyers), and it is harder to establish value. Your goal is to buy gold as a ready store of value, something that will rise in value as inflation (the overprinting of fiat currency such as the U.S. dollar) occurs and be a safe-haven asset in times of economic or political crisis. Jewelry does not fit the bill.

That leaves us with numismatic and bullion. Numismatic are gold coins for experienced coin collectors. The problem with numismatic gold coins is you are dealing with aspects of the coins beyond the intrinsic value of the gold itself in determining a fair price to buy and sell at. Issues such as rarity, date minted, condition, where it was minted, and historical significance can greatly alter the value of collector gold coins, making it very difficult to know if you are paying too much on the buy side or settling for too little on the sell side.

What you want to buy is bullion gold. **Bullion gold** is gold that is priced off the *gold spot price* tracked by the markets every day. It can be obtained as either coins or bars. Bullion coins and bars should have lower premium and commission costs above the market-quoted spot price for gold than jewelry or numismatic gold. Gold spot prices can be found posted frequently throughout the day at CNBC or Bloomberg TV or pretty much any website that tracks the major markets.

Should you buy gold bullion bars or gold bullion coins? There are problems with buying and owning bars. First, they are heavy, hard to ship, and hard to store. They can weigh as much as 400 ounces. If you are just starting out, this is an expensive way to get your feet wet, just from the sheer bulk of the transaction. Bars are useful if you have a ton of money and want to build a portfolio fast. But if you are a small-time gold investor, or want to start a gold portfolio slowly so you can learn as you go, gold coins are a better way to proceed. Gold bars are also a problem in that they cannot be easily broken up into pieces for small transactions. To liquidate your gold you have to sell at least an entire bar. The plus side of gold bars is you might be able to pay a lower commission per ounce on the transaction. Gold bars can be bought in 400-ounce, 100-ounce, 32.15-ounce (a kilo), or 1-ounce weights. Credit Suisse is one of the larger producers of gold bars.

That gets us to where you want to be, which is **buying gold bullion coins**. While commissions on coins can be slightly higher than on bars, it is worth it on the buy side for several reasons: First, there is a good chance you can get a good price on the sell side if you decide to liquidate. There is a lot of liquidity in gold bullion coins – lots of buyers and sellers. You can easily add to your portfolio, or easily sell a few coins, with little disruption to your portfolio – unlike if you had to sell gold bars – simply because you can control how many ounces you sell at a time. Another advantage to owning gold bullion coins is you will not have to deal with getting an assay – a scientific evaluation or measurement of the precise amount of gold in the coin. Coins are generally accepted without question.

The next issue is what weight gold coin should you buy? Your choices are gold coins that are less than one troy ounce, such as 1/10th or 1/4 or 1/2 a troy ounce, or full one-ounce gold coins. You will likely pay higher commissions on fractional-ounce gold coins than on one-ounce gold coins, so I suggest you buy one-ounce gold coins for the most part. There is a good reason to buy fractional gold coins though, and that is if you believe you will need to actually pay for food, energy, and other goods and services to live on with gold coins instead of the fiat currency we currently carry in our wallets. In that case, smaller fractional gold coins will be more convenient for buying inexpensive items, because in the precious metals money world, it will be very hard to get change for your one-ounce gold coins. But if you are just going to store your gold coins to exchange for some future new currency, or to have an asset that keeps pace with the rising cost of living, one-ounce gold coins should suffice. **The four most popular gold coins to own are the U.S. Gold Eagle, the U.S. Buffalo, the Canadian Maple Leaf, and the South African Krugerrand.**

Now we need to talk about karats. Gold bullion coins come in differing karats. U.S. Gold Eagles are 22 karats. South African Krugerrands are 22 karats. However, interestingly, the U.S. Buffalo gold bullion coin is 24 karats, as are the Canadian Maple Leaf coins. Twenty-four karats means the coin is 99.9 percent gold. Twenty-two karats means the coin is about 92 percent gold. Gold bars can also vary as far as their karats. A karat is a measure of the fineness of the gold content. Because gold is somewhat soft, coin minters mix an alloy, or another metal, with gold so the coins hold up. A 22-karat gold coin might consist of 1/12th copper and 11/12ths gold.

What does *troy ounce* mean? Gold and silver are sold by the troy ounce. A troy ounce is heavier than the ounce used to measure, for example, meat at the grocery store. A food-item ounce is 28.35 grams and a troy ounce is 31.1 grams. There is more gold in a troy ounce than there is meat in a grocery store ounce.

It is important to diversify to reduce risk in your portfolio. Ideally you will hold all four kinds of one-ounce gold coins mentioned above in your portfolio. You might want to buy a few coins per week or per month just to get a feel for the process, but also, very importantly, because gold prices can jump all over the place, and commissions can move around as well depending upon how difficult it is to fill an order. Supply and demand drives both.

By purchasing gold bullion coins a little at a time, you accomplish several benefits: You do not have to risk too much money in the hands of your gold broker at one time, so if there is a problem with their service you can make adjustments while your investment is still small. In the coming Economic Ice Age, a lot of good businesses will suffer and might close down. By doing lots of smaller transactions with gold coins, your exposure to a possible failed transaction is reduced. Another benefit is that of cost-averaging your purchases. In other words, if the spot price of gold drops, you get to buy gold coins cheaper. Then, as it goes back up, the value of all the coins you hold rises. Cost-averaging is a long-term investing tool to improve overall investment returns. It applies to gold and silver coin purchases as well. A third benefit is that by purchasing a few coins at a time, regularly, over a long period of time, it is easier to manage delivery and storage issues.

What should you know about buying silver bullion coins? While you can buy silver bars, the same problems exist as with gold bars. If you do buy silver bars, the most popular is *generic silver rounds* (or *bars*). There are 1,000-ounce (68 pound) bars, used to settle futures contracts on the New York Mercantile Exchange. There are also 100-troy-ounce silver bars and 10-ounce silver bars.

What you want to buy are silver coins. Before you dismiss silver thinking you should only buy gold, think about this fact: There is over twice as much gold above ground throughout the world than silver; silver is rarer than gold. Silver has been a monetary unit of exchange for thousands of years. While silver's spot price is currently a fraction per troy ounce of gold's, the future for silver should be bright based simply on supply issues.

There are two main types of silver bullion coins you can purchase: officially government-minted one-ounce coins or officially government-minted *junk silver* bags of coins. Again, you don't want to have to get an assay when dealing in silver. That is why you want to purchase only *officially government-minted* silver coins.

One approach is to buy one-troy-ounce **silver dollar coins. The most popular is the U.S. Silver Eagle bullion coin, which the U.S. government started minting in 1986. It contains 99.9 percent silver.** Other popular silver coins include the Canadian Silver Maple Leaf and the Austrian Silver Philharmonic.

Another approach to buying silver coins is to buy what is known as *junk silver*. It is probably inappropriately named as there is a lot of value here. These are officially U.S. government-minted silver coins below a one-dollar denomination that were minted through 1964. They are dimes, quarters, and half dollars. Their silver content is 90 percent. Many of you (those over fifty-five years young) are familiar with these coins because they were rampant when you were growing up. You probably used them as a kid to buy ice cream, soda from a machine, or a pack of baseball cards, or to make a telephone call at a phone booth. You know, the coins you could kick yourself for not hanging on to and storing back when you were a kid.

The most popular way to buy junk silver is to buy a 55-pound bag. This means you are buying $1,000 in face value of silver coins – 715 troy ounces of silver. The cost for this bag depends on what the spot price per troy ounce is for silver on the day you purchase it, plus commissions. Commissions, or premiums, vary depending on supply and demand for junk silver. When buying junk silver, it is important to understand that you are not buying coins with numismatic value per se. Most of these coins are in poor condition, worn down from heavy usage over time. But that is okay, as they are worth the spot price silver bullion value. They were at one time government-issued silver coins, and the government no longer mints them, so they could become more scarce as time goes on, meaning they should gain value given their limited supply. You will not need an assay before buying or selling them since they are U.S. government minted. The most desirable junk silver coins are the half dollars, then the quarters, with dimes the least in demand. However, if you believe there will come a day when in order to buy goods and services you will need to pay with silver or gold, the smaller coins will be important because it might be hard to get change if you are buying something relatively inexpensive. Maybe a loaf of bread will go for one silver dime instead of three fiat dollars. We don't quite know exactly what we are going to be dealing with in the coming Economic Ice Age, so having some junk silver could prove to be important.

How do you buy gold and silver bullion coins? You now are ready to buy. Let's say you have decided to buy two U.S. Gold Eagle dollars and one U.S. Silver Eagle dollar to start your precious metals portfolio.

The next step is to find a reputable metals brokerage firm from which to buy your gold and silver. You do not have to use a broker; you could work with a local business that trades gold and silver. But assuming you do not know a local dealer or one whom you trust, you will work with a broker, one who might be located several hundred or several thousand miles from you. That is okay. Distance does not matter.

Warning: You probably do not want to buy gold on the internet or from a gold dealer who advertises heavily on TV, in spite of the fact that they are easy to find. They have to cover the cost of those ads. And you'll have to be careful about commissions and the procedure for delivery of the genuine metal.

You want a reputable brokerage that will educate you, build trust with you, charge fair commissions, ship quickly, stand by the gold it delivered, and buy it back from you should you want to sell.

Call your reputable precious metals broker and tell them what you want to buy. If you have already set up an account with them and sent them a check to cover future purchases, and that check has cleared and you have good funds in your account with them, you can begin the order process in which they will buy the coins and charge your account. If you have not set up an account, you will have to wire transfer the money to pay for the coins and commissions before the order is given. When you call your broker, they are first going to check the current market price for the coins. If you agree to that price, after checking the spot price on TV or the internet yourself and making sure the price is close to the spot price, you tell your broker to go ahead and buy the coins for you. The broker then locks in the price, meaning the broker has bought the coins on your behalf at the price quoted to you. The broker then charges your account for the cost of the coins plus commissions they are charging to do the transaction. Once the transaction has been locked in, you are no longer able to change your mind.

Now you can expect delivery of the coins. You want to make sure your broker is shipping the coins registered, tracked, and fully insured, using either USPS or UPS or some similar reputable transport service. You want your broker to ship your package such that delivery requires your signature. You don't want to worry about it being delivered to your neighbor's house or dropped off at your home and stolen. You can even ask that it be kept at the post office so you can safely pick it up there.

How do you maintain privacy when buying precious metals coins? Believe it or not, paying with cash or money orders are not more private ways to pay than with a personal check or wire transfer. Why? Because **The Bank Secrecy Act of 1970** (or **BSA**, or otherwise known as the **Currency and Foreign Transactions Reporting Act**) requires that banks and businesses file reports to the government for cash or money-order transactions greater than $10,000, and to maintain a log of cash transactions greater than $3,000 accumulated per day. This means you actually have more privacy paying for precious metals coins with a personal check or wire transfer.

How do you store your precious metals coins? You have a few options. One is to place your coins in a safe deposit box in a safe, local bank. With the coming Economic Ice Age, you have to ask the question "How safe will that bank be?" Some banks are going to fail just as we saw back in the Great Recession of 2007 through 2009. Why should that concern you? Because if the bank that you have your coins stored in fails, you can lose access to your safe deposit box for an extended period of time. Another issue you have to think about if you plan to store your coins in a bank safe deposit box is that if you have personal financial troubles – and that is a possibility during the coming Economic Ice Age – it is possible that the contents of your safe deposit box will be seized by the authority you owe money to. A court order against you could result in such a seizure. The contents of bank safe deposit boxes are strictly regulated by the government. Some items cannot be legally stored in them, and they can be sealed upon the owner's death.

Another option is to store your physical gold and silver in one of the many big storage facilities in Delaware. One such facility is Diamond State Depository in Wilmington, Delaware.

A third option is a home safe. The risk here is that the safe could be stolen. Linda Gorman, Vice President of Resource Consultants, Inc. in Tempe, Arizona, who has been a precious metals broker for over thirty years, has some interesting insights about home storage:

> A home safe is good to have. Most robberies occur in the bedroom. You might have a small safe in a closet with some cash, jewelry, and a copy of insurance papers or something. Then if you are robbed, the scoundrel might just take that with him and go away. Keep the bulk of your valuables in another area or property in

something too big and heavy to carry off. A fire safe TL30 is supposed to withstand attack for 30 minutes with professional tools. Most robbers would rather take jewelry or electronics that they can get in and out with in a hurry. Years ago, there was a product called "The Midnight Gardener" (aptly named Midnight Gardener because people would put their valuables in it and bury it in the back yard). What this item consisted of was a piece of PVC pipe with end caps and sealant. Be careful if you use something like this because you do not want to risk getting your gold and silver wet or having someone with a metal detector scanning your property. These pipes are sometimes tucked into other places such as heating ducts. Empty paint buckets in the back of the garage are other ways we have heard of storing your metal. Again, I cannot stress this enough, do not put all your eggs in one basket!

A clever way to store precious metals is to disguise them. Hide them inside everyday items such as DVD movie cases or three-ring notebooks. Or build a false wall and place a small safe behind it.

Linda Gorman also has another warning about storage:

Do not buy your metals from the same company that stores your metals too. I cannot tell you how many horror stories we have heard from clients who in years past purchased their metal from a company who supplied storage for their clients. Some of these companies were ill managed and went out of business after robbing from Peter to pay Paul with their clients' metals. Those clients never were able to collect their metals and even though the company owners did jail time, it is small consolation when your money is gone and a trust is broken.

How much should you pay in commissions for your gold and silver coins? While commissions are all over the place, and it can depend on how difficult it is to acquire the coins for you – that is, supply and demand issues – you should not be paying more than 3 to 10 percent commissions on gold and silver coin purchases, with 5 percent being the average. This is where you can get into trouble if you are not dealing with a reputable broker. You can check the spot price of the metal per ounce, which is easy to find as it is flashed about every few minutes on the television screen on CNBC TV, and compare that to what the broker is quoting you. The cost for coins should be a bit higher than the spot price, which is fine. But whatever else they are charging you is the commission they get. You want this to be reasonable. Don't flinch at paying commissions up to 10 percent because brokers provide a valuable service, making it possible for you to accumulate coins for the future – for that day if and when currency or inflation mega-trouble comes.

There are some pitfalls to watch out for when buying gold and silver coins. You have to watch out for counterfeit coins. This is why you should not buy your coins off the internet or in answer to some overbearing TV ad. Which brings us to another: You have to be careful in buying newly minted coins because some unscrupulous brokers and dealers charge commissions (premiums) of 50 to 100 percent on newly minted coins on the basis that they are graded as numismatic "first strike" collectibles. They buy the coins for 3 percent over spot price from the U.S. Mint and sell them for 50 to 100 percent over spot price. This is one of the worst scams out there according to Linda Gorman:

You might have seen advertisements for Graded Mint state Gold or Silver Eagles. We will have them for you but we do not recommend them. These are newly minted coins. They are all mint state. You are paying a higher commission to have them sent off to PCGS or NGC for grading. Basically, no matter how much they are romanced, they are still graded just bullion. The (high) premium you pay does not usually hold when you sell them back in the market. There are times when we have seen them available for close to the raw coin price.

Linda and Pat Gorman operate Resource Consultants, Inc. in Tempe, Arizona. They have been in the metals business for over thirty years. They are metals brokers whom you can contact at 1-800-494-4149. Their address is 6139 S. Rural Rd., Ste. 103, Tempe, AZ 85283. Their website address is www.BuySilverNow. com. They offer a newsletter eleven times per year. Linda is Vice President and her husband, Pat, hosts the longest running financial radio program in Phoenix, *Hard Money Watch*. Their motto is "Education before Acquisition." They have hosted the annual Wealth Protection Conference for nearly two decades, and come highly recommended by many financial experts throughout the U.S. I would like to thank Linda for her contribution to this section of the book.

If you would like to learn more about how to buy physical gold and silver, I recommend the book by my friend Paul Mladjenovic titled *Precious Metals Investing for Dummies*, copyright 2008, Wiley Publishing, Inc.

Also, I would like to thank my good friend Roger Wiegand, who writes a weekly precious metals newsletter at www. tradertracks.com.

CHAPTER EIGHT

Strategy Three: U.S. Treasuries and Other Securities

For those of you who are novices in investing, U.S. Treasury securities, commonly known as Treasuries, are direct debt obligations of the United States of America. The U.S. guarantees repayment based on the terms stated in the Treasury issue you choose. Treasuries have various terms ranging from a week to thirty years. The longer the term of the Treasury you purchase, the greater the chance that unfortunate events will occur that could reduce the value of the Treasury obligation you own. (I will cover those risks below.)

Treasuries can be purchased through a brokerage firm or directly from the U.S. government. Treasury notes and Treasury bonds – those Treasuries with terms of a year or more – pay a coupon interest amount equal to the stated interest rate for the security. For Treasury bills (Treasuries with terms of less than a year), there is no interest payment; you buy the bill at a discount of the par amount you get paid back at maturity, the difference generating your return. Notes and bills pay half their interest twice a year. Treasuries are in very high demand, meaning there are always willing buyers, and they have excellent liquidity, so you should have no problem converting them to cash by selling before maturity.

If you had to concentrate your wealth in any one investment item, U.S. Treasuries would be it. This is especially the case for those of you who have wealth in the millions, but also true for anyone who wants premium safety for their nest egg, including amounts in the tens and hundreds of thousands. However, I would not go long-term in Treasuries; I would stick with short-term Treasury bills or notes for two reasons: The first is the risk of depreciation due to interest-rate risk – the risk that interest rates will rise after you purchase your Treasuries. And the second is the risk of credit downgrade.

Let's talk about these two risks. First, **interest-rate risk**. We are approaching the Economic Ice Age during a period of historically low interest rates, with the highest-rated short-term securities (maturing in less than one year) yielding near zero. In fact, as this book is being written, you cannot even find a 1 percent return unless you buy a Treasury that matures after five years. That means if you buy Treasuries, and interest rates rise, the value of the Treasuries will decline. This is because the interest rate sought by potential buyers will be greater than the interest rate of your Treasuries. If you need to sell your Treasuries before maturity, you will receive less than what you paid. The longer the term for the Treasury you bought, the greater the decline in the Treasury security's value should interest rates rise.

What can you do to protect yourself from interest-rate risk? The protective compensating strategy is to buy very-short-term Treasuries. This has two benefits: One, the amount of devaluation in the Treasury if interest rates rise is less for a short-term instrument than a long-term instrument due to the time-value of money and discounting-present-value mathematics. Two, upon maturity you get 100 percent of your money back no matter what interest rates do, so if you need money it is just a short wait until your Treasury matures. An interesting strategy is to *ladder* maturities – have a series of Treasury securities that mature at different times (a ladder), so that once a week, once a month, or once every three months – whatever you think your cash requirements will be – a portion of your Treasury portfolio will mature at full value (par), providing the cash you need.

Let's look at **credit risk. This is the risk that the U.S. government will not pay you back your money or will fail to pay you back when coupon or principal payments are due.** When you buy a Treasury, you are in essence lending the U.S. government money. A U.S. Treasury therefore has the full faith and credit of the U.S. government behind it. As long as the United States exists, it promises to pay you back, and on time. I suggest investing in U.S. Treasuries because in my opinion the United States of America has the strongest military, the most stable political structure, and a proven track record, and therefore provides the highest probability of repayment of your money, on time, and upon maturity. Even if the rating services downgrade the ratings of U.S. government securities due to events like weak tax receipts, large deficits, too much Treasury debt outstanding in relation to one year's GDP, political stalemates, etc., they are your best bet for getting repaid both the interest you are expecting and the principal you originally invested.

The nice thing about U.S. Treasuries, which makes them different from cash, is that your entire investment in Treasuries is 100 percent guaranteed by the sovereign nation of the United States of America. When you buy Treasuries, the U.S. does not just guarantee repayment for a portion of the investment, but for all of it. In the case of cash in the bank, you have only the guarantee from the FDIC, an agency of the U.S. Government, the funds of which can become depleted if the banks it insures go belly up. Widespread bank failures put a strain on the FDIC fund, meaning the FDIC has to go back to the U.S. Congress to refund the kitty that is used to repay you should the bank you have your cash in go down the toilet. In other words, there is a middle man between you and the United States – the FDIC. Further, there are limitations on how much of your cash is guaranteed by the FDIC. After the 2007 to 2009 recession, the amount was raised from $100,000 to $250,000 per account holder, which is sufficient for most households and small businesses. But if you have more than $250,000, you are at risk of losing all amounts above $250,000 you have on deposit should your bank become insolvent (fail to meet its required minimum capital levels). Something that might be startling to those of you who are unfamiliar with the banking industry is that many banks typically fund only 5 percent of their assets with capital; the remaining 95 percent is funded with debt (deposits and borrowings). If more than 5 percent of their assets become worthless, the bank becomes insolvent and will be closed down by government regulators. That is not much of a cushion if you are going to place more than $250,000 in your name in a bank. It does not matter if you have three separate accounts; if they are all in the same account-holder name, only $250,000 is insured by the FDIC.

One way to get around this $250,000 limitation is to spread your money around in different banks. This allows you to get a full $250,000 of FDIC protection at each of those banks. Be sure that the bank you put your money in is in fact a member of the Federal Deposit Insurance Corporation! Some online banks are not. Another way to get around it is to deposit your money in separate accounts at the same bank that are in different account-holder names. For example, let's say you have $750,000 in cash that you want to have in one bank. If you are married, you can carve the money into three $250,000 accounts, one in your name alone, one in your spouse's name alone, and a third in the joint name of you and your spouse. That gets you FDIC insurance coverage – a theoretical guarantee by the United States – for $750,000 in one bank.

There is legislative risk with FDIC insurance. The risk is that the U.S. Congress will pass legislation that changes the way FDIC insurance works. For example, it might reduce the amount of coverage from $250,000 back to something less, or change the quality of the U.S. guarantee. Since the viability of the U.S. economy depends on a fully functioning banking system with lending as the key catalyst for economic growth, and the raw material for that lending – customer deposits – is a critical and necessary component, it is essential and therefore likely that the U.S. should not mess around with people's trust in banks, and should keep the FDIC insurance program going strong. However, it is important to understand that FDIC insurance is not as safe and secure as U.S. Treasuries, which are a direct obligation of the sovereign U.S., and that there are limitations with FDIC and no limitations with Treasuries.

How you buy Treasuries, from whom, and where they are stored is important to consider prior to the Economic Ice Age. At its inception you will still be able to conduct business with most regulated and reputable banks and brokerage firms without incurring much risk. However, as the economic collapse deepens and widens, we will start to see out-of-the-blue failures that pose a couple of risks to you, the investor. One, you might see frauds, computer failures, and accounting irregularities, and it might take you a long time to prove to regulators who oversee and take over these institutions what you own, how much of your securities or cash they hold, and what you are entitled to. If your funds were misappropriated, meaning they spent your money, then you might not get anything back, especially if you invested in anything other than Treasuries or FDIC-insured cash. You might have to hire a lawyer, which can be expensive; you might need money sooner than it comes back after the cleanup of the failed institution is completed. So **as the economy worsens, you should spread your money around.** Put your Treasuries and FDIC-insured cash in many different banks and brokerages. This will increase the odds that you can access at least some of your money when you need it.

As the economic depression matures (worsens), you might want to think about moving your Treasuries to an account at one of the twelve Federal Reserve Banks. You can buy from them and they will keep your Treasuries safe for you. You go to one of these banks, open up a securities account, and purchase Treasuries directly from the U.S. government through the Federal Reserve, which is the bank for the U.S. government and is essentially part of the U.S. government. Do this when you start to see major investment banking (brokerage) houses fail. Transacting with the Federal Reserve is less convenient than simply buying and selling and storing Treasuries with a local or online brokerage firm, but this is the step to take to protect your wealth just before confidence in our major financial institutions is lost.

There are many other fixed-income securities to choose from when investing your money, such as corporate notes and bonds and municipal notes and bonds. Here is the problem: These securities have far greater credit risk than U.S. Treasuries do. If you buy a corporate note from a large company, you do not have a guarantee from the United States of America; you are hoping the company whose security you purchased will remain solvent and pay you back. And during the coming Economic Ice Age, especially as it deepens, many large corporations will fail and you could lose your entire investment, or their ratings will drop so low as their earnings decline that the value of your security will drop substantially before it matures, leaving you stuck with an illiquid asset, since you may not want to take a huge loss by selling it early. You might be tempted to buy corporate notes and bonds because the yields they return are presented as much higher than Treasuries. However, the risk that the company will go down the toilet is far greater than with a Treasury, and you can lose everything by chasing the higher yields that corporate notes and bonds tempt you with. Stay away from corporate securities once the Economic Ice Age begins.

As for municipal securities, here is my take: The nice thing about municipal securities is that the interest you are paid is free from federal income tax per the IRS code as this book is being written. If the trend toward raising income tax rates continues, increasing the tax savings and benefits of owning municipal notes and bonds, it will be very tempting for high-income and high-net-worth individuals to park a significant amount of their money in municipals. There is a legislative risk that Congress will change the tax code and no longer allow municipal security interest income to be tax free. Municipal securities can be seen as a tax shelter for the rich; as the trend toward socialism spreads in the United States, the tax code might be changed to remove this tax shelter.

There is also credit risk with municipals. For example, as this book is being written, the city of Detroit, Michigan, filed for bankruptcy. Not all municipals are alike. Some are issued by small local communities, boroughs, towns, cities, townships, parishes, etc. in low-income areas where the income available to be taxed can decline, or is already small, thus raising the risk that the municipality might not be able to pay you back. As the economy worsens, tax receipts are going to decline in many locales. If you own municipal securities, you are relying on the taxing authority of the wage earners in that district to repay you. Then there are school district municipal notes and bonds. Personally, I like these better, on the theory that schools today are given such a high priority by voters that taxes will always be raised sufficient to repay debts and operate schools. But again, even with school district municipal securities, there is interest-rate risk and legislative risk. And if the mood of the populace changes and schools are not able to raise taxes further, there is also credit risk that is far greater than with U.S. Treasuries.

Some municipal securities have credit insurance attached to them, through which the financial strength of the insurer guarantees part or all of the security should the municipality be unable to pay the stated principal or interest on time. However, it is private companies that insure municipalities, not a U.S. agency, and they do not maintain sufficient reserves to handle a total economic collapse. So be careful about relying on these credit enhancements. Look primarily to the strength of the underlying municipality when making such an investment decision.

For example, the Ambac Financial Group, Inc. (Ambac) was one of these credit insurers, and held a pristine AAA rating for years, meaning any municipality that had bought Ambac's guarantee for bonds it was issuing for sale also received a AAA rating from the major credit rating agencies such as Standard & Poor's (S&P), Moody's, or Fitch. But Ambac got slammed by the 2007 subprime mortgage crisis, and the ratings agencies gradually lowered their rating on Ambac from AAA down to junk status from 2008 through 2010. Finally, on November 8th, 2010, Ambac filed for Chapter 11 bankruptcy. Prior to 2007, if you bought and owned a municipal bond with an underlying credit rating of A, but the credit rating was enhanced by Ambac's guarantee to AAA, you paid more for the bond than had it not been insured by Ambac; you paid more for the enhanced rating. Then as the Great Recession unfolded and Ambac's credit rating fell below AAA, the rating on your municipal bond also fell and therefore the value of your bond fell, meaning you then owned a bond at a loss. In this case, the rating on your bond fell to the rating of the underlying municipality – to A. (Note: AAA is the highest rating, then AA, then A, then BBB).

In conclusion, once the Economic Ice Age starts, I prefer U.S. Treasuries and FDIC-insured deposits over corporate and municipal securities.

INVESTMENT LADDER

A Winning Strategy for Investing in Fixed-Income Securities

For many fixed-income (bills, notes, and bonds) investors, capital gains are the ultimate objective, with double-digit returns highly desirable. To achieve these objectives, investors buy notes and bonds when they think interest rates are going down, and sell notes and bonds – or shorten the maturities of the ones they own substantially – when they think rates are going up (the operative word here being *think*). To decide when to buy and when to sell notes and bonds, investors often consult with their brokers. The broker's advice 90 percent of the time? "Buy!" And that is natural since brokers make more money when more people are buying than are selling. It is human nature to be optimistic if you are a broker and your living depends on selling securities. The point here is to be very careful about the terms of fixed-income securities in which you invest. You are on your own, or should get independent financial guidance about the future path for interest rates from a source independent from that from whom you buy the securities.

After a while, an investor who happily took a broker's advice to buy might start to feel some anxiety. As interest rates rise and fixed-income security prices fall, the value of recently purchased securities declines. In times like this, the temptation is to sell, for surely tomorrow's prices (moving in the inverse direction of interest rates) will be even lower. The broker doesn't try too hard to change the investor's mind; after all, a trade is a trade.

The long and short of this is that the investor has probably bought fixed-income securities when prices were high and sold when prices were low – just the opposite of what was desired. When a portfolio overemphasizes gains and returns, with little regard for other reasons for investing, it quickly evolves into nothing more than a trading account, driven like a boat on the high seas of emotion. Trading volume runs high because the portfolio is churned frequently in search of elusive gains. Administering this sort of trading portfolio requires considerable time and, I guarantee you, many a sleepless night. If trading is what you want to do, you should be studying technical market analysis charts that forecast price and interest-rate moves. That requires expertise or being plugged in to a technical market analysis service for their expertise such as we provide at **www.technicalindicatorindex.com**.

Objectives of Portfolios

Investors should not look at their portfolios of securities as isolated profit centers. Instead, investment practices should be developed with a mind toward managing risks, meeting contingencies, and optimizing returns. A well-managed investment portfolio should have the following objectives:

(1) to provide a well-diversified portfolio of safe, credit-worthy assets

(2) to offer a dependable and continuous source of cash, and to provide a secondary, indirect source of liquidity (which can be pledged as collateral for borrowings, for example)

(3) to manage market value risks, both interest-rate risk and credit risk

(4) to provide a steady stream of dependable earnings (such as coupon interest payments)

(5) to provide capital gains opportunities

How can a portfolio accomplish all of these objectives? Aren't liquidity (the ability to convert your security to cash quickly) and earnings mutually exclusive goals? For cash liquidity, don't you need to stay short-term – at the low end of the earnings curve? And where do you invest to minimize market-value-fluctuation risk?

Investment portfolio management is as much an art as it is a science. **I would like to suggest an approach that is nearly perfect for accomplishing all of the above objectives.** The approach is fairly simple to understand and to administer, but it requires a great deal of discipline and cash, and works best with an upward-sloping yield curve (short-term yields are lower than long-term yields, a condition that happens to occur most of the time). You also have to be willing to stay with the strategy in the face of some early paper losses.

This strategy, called the *ladder approach*, allows you to choose various types of securities investments. Thus, if tax management is a concern, you can mix in some municipal notes or bonds. If earnings are a high priority, you can choose corporate bonds over U.S. Treasuries or U.S. agencies. If you own a considerable number of high-risk assets – for example equities, choosing U.S. Treasuries makes sense for diversifying credit risk. If you are concerned about the coming Economic Ice Age, stick with just Treasuries.

Example: Let's say you have $1 million to invest. The first thing you should ask yourself is how much cash you need for temporary emergencies. What if you lost your job? You might need a couple of years worth of money to live on before you find a comparable job. So let's say $200,000 is off limits, leaving $800,000 for investment.

Next ask yourself how much cash you would like to see coming in (maturing) each month. Let's say you want $20,000 each month. Then you should divide the $800,000 available for investment by $20,000, giving you forty blocks of investments. You will be making forty investments of $20,000, each with a different maturity.

Next, you need to make a risk assessment of where we are in the interest-rate cycle. Are rates at historic lows, meaning the probability is high that interest rates will rise, perhaps substantially? If so, weight the distribution of maturities toward shorter terms. Still, there is always the risk that rates could go lower – perhaps due to an equity market collapse or another terrorist attack, which would produce a *flight to quality* in which U.S. Treasuries become the investment of first choice for many fearful investors. So you'll want to have some longer-term maturities in place as well, maybe a few pieces with two-year terms. Once interest rates start to rise, you can reinvest maturing cash at the long end of the ladder, and if interest rates rise significantly, you can start pushing your longest-term investments a little further into the future than when you started the portfolio. This gives you more yield and sets you up for some capital gains should rates decline again. For example, maybe at the start your longest-term Treasury was two years. If interest rates rise, the next time you have cash maturing at the short end of the ladder you can reinvest it at the two-year, three-months term. If rates continue to rise, your next cash reinvestment can be at the two-year, six-months term, and so on.

You now must determine what types of securities to purchase. If you already hold assets with significant credit risk, perhaps equities that generate no earnings such as start-up technology firms; or you own bonds of a firm whose credit ratings keep slipping; or Fannie Mae or Freddie Mac – issues with increasing derivatives risk and risk of downgrades or default should the economy head south; you will want to choose very-low-credit-risk issues such as U.S. Treasuries. However, to enhance yield a bit, you might select some high-grade corporate securities or maybe some municipal general obligation securities, although, again, once the Economic Ice Age starts, I would stick to U.S. Treasuries.

You map out your security ladder, investing $20,000 in issues maturing in forty different periods spread across short and medium terms, perhaps from one month to five years. (However, under the current economic and interest-rate climate I would keep the longest maturity at two years.) To keep the average term at two-and-a-half years for starters, if you purchase a security maturing next month, you would need to purchase another one maturing five years from now. Your portfolio should be skewed toward the short term at the beginning. That way, if market rates rise, you have the chance to reinvest a good portion of your funds at the higher rates.

How gains climb: As an example, look at the sample ladder portfolio below. Next month you will reinvest the first block of money maturing – the first $20,000 – at the high end of the yield curve – the sixty-month yield of 3.50%, replacing a 1.50% security with a 3.50% security without changing the overall average term of the portfolio. If this process continues, you will eventually have an entire portfolio of securities yielding an overall 3.50% instead of the current 2.25%, yet the average term will be the same. Keep in mind that the current interest-rate environment is far lower than the interest rates used in this theoretical portfolio example.

INVESTMENT STARTING LADDER

Month Maturing	Security		Yield	Month Maturing	Security		Yield
1	T Note	$20,000	1.50%	31	T Note	$20,000	2.75%
2	T Note	$20,000	1.55%	32			
3	T Note	$20,000	1.60%	33	T Note	$20,000	2.80%
4	T Note	$20,000	1.65%	34			
5	T Note	$20,000	1.70%	35	T Note	$20,000	2.85%
6	T Note	$20,000	1.75%	36			
7	T Note	$20,000	1.80%	37	T Note	$20,000	2.90%
8	T Note	$20,000	1.85%	38			
9	T Note	$20,000	1.90%	39	T Note	$20,000	2.95%
10	T Note	$20,000	1.95%	40			
11	T Note	$20,000	2.00%	41	T Note	$20,000	3.00%
12	T Note	$20,000	2.05%	42			
13	T Note	$20,000	2.10%	43	T Note	$20,000	3.05%
14	T Note	$20,000	2.15%	44			
15	T Note	$20,000	2.20%	45	T Note	$20,000	3.10%
16	T Note	$20,000	2.25%	46			
17	T Note	$20,000	2.30%	47	T Note	$20,000	3.15%
18	T Note	$20,000	2.35%	48			
19	T Note	$20,000	2.40%	49	T Note	$20,000	3.20%
20	T Note	$20,000	2.45%	50			
21	T Note	$20,000	2.50%	51	T Note	$20,000	3.25%
22				52			
23	T Note	$20,000	2.55%	53	T Note	$20,000	3.30%
24				54			
25	T Note	$20,000	2.60%	55	T Note	$20,000	3.35%
26				56			
27	T Note	$20,000	2.65%	57	T Note	$20,000	3.40%
28				58			
29	T Note	$20,000	2.70%	59	T Note	$20,000	3.50%
30				60			

In the long run you will see some nice capital gains at the short end of the portfolio as the 3.50% securities roll down onto the short-term maturity rungs. The long end of the portfolio will realize capital gains during periods of falling interest rates, which is exactly one of your goals. During a rising-rate period, liquidity from the long end of the ladder is not needed, so you can weather normal market depreciation and wait out the rising-rate cycle. Worst case, you hold these issues until maturity and cash them in at par. And if you have extraordinary needs for profits, even in a rising-rate period capital gains should be available at the short end of the ladder.

Many wrinkles can be added to this approach. If you end up with 25 percent gains in the entire portfolio, it might make sense to sell the whole thing, build up cash, and start again, figuring interest rates will rise soon enough that the portfolio's new lower startup yield can be improved within a reasonable period of time. Another option is to purchase an additional quantity of securities because you have extra cash on hand, or to take advantage of specific yield-curve opportunities (the curve isn't always rising, often it inverts). Here you simply fill in previously empty slots in the ladder maturities. Or perhaps you want to cash out of notes and bonds because it's time to rebalance all of your assets and increase your position in equities (perhaps equity price-to-earnings ratios (PEs) have fallen to bargain levels, maybe between 6X and 10X on blue chips, with dividend yields floating above 5 percent). However, once the Economic Ice Age begins, I would only hold equities in a speculative or market-timing, carefully controlled, risk-managed segment of my total portfolio, using expert buy and sell signals from reliable technical market analysis indicators such as we provide at **www.technicalindicatorindex.com**.

You must have patience when starting. You might initially be under water if interest rates start rising just as you begin the investment ladder. But the $20,000 maturing next month can be reinvested at a higher rate. Even if interest rates don't fall soon, time alone – combined with the natural upward slope of the yield curve – will bring the portfolio above water. Gains will appear, yields will be high, and liquidity will be flowing steadily from periodic coupon payments, the reinvestment of coupon payments having a compounding effect on yield.

I think you'll find this to be a terrific conservative investment strategy for turbulent economic times, albeit the interest-rate environment during which you start this ladder portfolio might differ from the above example.

CHAPTER NINE

Strategy Four:
Multiple Income Sources

This chapter is about wisdom. The Economic Ice Age is going to start with our nation's job picture already bleak. That will make matters ten times worse, with trouble coming much faster once the Economic Ice Age begins than if we presently sat at full employment. The goal here is to protect yourself against unexpected loss of income through no fault of your own. You want to be positioned so that if you lose your job, you have other sources of income to sustain your lifestyle. This protection can be achieved with a little ingenuity and some guts. It involves putting yourself in a position to be your own boss in at least one financial endeavor.

During the Economic Ice Age, jobs will be lost – a ton of jobs – and with them family income. Working for "the man" is not going to assure you of anything. You will not be able to trust your employer for job security. The corporate cult will eat you alive and spit you out. Dog eat dog like you have never seen before. There will be little loyalty.

Look at all the cutbacks in jobs we have seen in the past decade from two recessions. Right now 22.2 million good folks out of a total work force of 143.5 million are unemployed. Of the employed, 21.5 million work for either local, state, or federal governments. Are those jobs safe given the fiscal deficits being run up now? No. Our total population stands at 315 million. On average, every person working is supporting at least one other person. The repercussions of more job losses are that not only will more households suffer, but the economy will suffer as consumer spending declines.

None of these employment numbers addresses quality jobs, family- or household-supporting jobs, jobs that pay more than minimum wage. Forty-eight million people are on food stamps, but there are 22 million unemployed.[1] That speaks to the high number of people working but stuck in low-wage jobs. It is only going to get worse – much worse.

There are 79 million families in the United States. In 2012 there were 1.2 million bankruptcies and 747,000 foreclosures.[1] The Economic Ice Age will be hitting us at a time when we are not strong. The U.S. and world economies were just beaten down by two recessions in the past ten years. Now another one is coming, far worse than before. It is as if the same locale were hit by two hurricanes the size of Sandy and Katrina, yet another one is coming that is even more powerful than they were, and we are still not back on our feet from the previous storms.

So income is going to be the challenge. Even if you have money, where are you going to get an acceptable rate of return on a safe investment? Bank deposits? Interest rates are pathetic, less than 1 percent for short-term deposits. Treasury securities? No again – less than 1 percent for short-term securities. Interest income is essentially non-existent. This has been killing, and it will continue to destroy senior citizen and retiree income. Stocks are going to drop. Real estate is going to drop. Jobs are going to be lost. Quality jobs are going by the wayside. Not good. What do you do?

You should think about coming up with three generators of income from three independent, separate sources. There are many ways to accomplish this, but the idea is that you want to have backup in case one of your sources of income is temporarily or permanently lost.

If you have a good job, great. That is one source. If your spouse has a good job, great. That is another source. But in speaking with bankers, I know of situations in which a good loan became a bad loan overnight because not just one, but both spouses unexpectedly lost their jobs. It happens. That means you need a third source of income, maybe even a fourth. Here are some ideas:

1. a part-time job away from home (though there is the danger of burnout and damage to your family life)

2. a part-time job that you do at home (here is where you can and should get creative; we will explore this below)

3. rental income

4. disciplined, controlled, speculative investing with only a small segment of your portfolio (we will cover this in the next chapter)

Let's first examine adding a part-time job away from home. It's likely to be something more menial than your day job. It could be working in retail or a trade such as painter, seamstress, handyman, or car mechanic – something for evenings and weekends. There is a lack of quality workmanship in many trades, especially since the last recession when permanent construction jobs were lost and some of the best craftsmen reengineered themselves into new careers. You can make good money part time if you are willing to climb a ladder, cut hair, or give pedicures or massages. Some of these jobs require licenses or training. That is okay. Get 'er done. If you look around at the millions of illegal immigrants doing manual labor in this country, it shows you there are job opportunities. Maybe you can start a small part-time business and hire others to do the actual work while you manage it. Cleaning houses, schools, churches, post offices. Not glamorous work, but work nonetheless. Nobody who knows you at your day job has to know. Truthfully, they probably won't care that much because they also know that at any given time anyone can lose their day job. Loyalty is a thing of the past in most companies even though most CEOs would deny this truth to the death.

Here is a key point: Get independent. If you can start your own business, whether outside the home or something you do at home, do it. Be your own boss. Get incorporated. It is not that expensive and provides legal protection for your endeavor. I know a guy who runs a snow-plowing business. He doesn't own a plow, doesn't do any plowing. He finds customers by placing ads on local store bulletin boards, word of mouth, and a few ads in the paper. He subcontracts the work to a seasonally unemployed landscaper who needs work in the winter, has the plow and truck, but doesn't have the entrepreneurial spirit or extrovert personality to find customers. They split the fee. The same can be done with chopped fireplace wood. Or tree trimming. Or gutter cleaning. Or power-washing. Or AAA flat tire repairs. Are you a teacher? How about starting an evening tutoring business. Target customers who can afford the service – children of upper- and middle-income families. Are you musically inclined? Give lessons in the evenings to school kids. Become a teacher online for a home-schooling program. Create extracurricular programs for home-schooled children. They need music, art, physical education, drama, and foreign-language instruction that is hard for a parent to teach at home. Homeschoolers need social activities. Set up programs for these intelligent and eager-to-learn kids. Do something that produces income for you and where you are the boss and nobody can fire you.

Maybe working a second job from home is a better fit for you. Think about what you are good at. You have one of the easiest and most efficient delivery systrems ever created at your fingertips; the internet puts you in touch with the entire globe. You can set up a website, set up a merchant account to collect payments from credit cards or through a payment system such as PayPal, and sell something to the entire world. You can sell a service or a product to anyone anywhere. You can sell items on eBay or Amazon.com. Become a picker of old books, movies, records, collectables, or specialties and sell them as used items at one of these websites. Clean out your attic or help your neighbor clean out theirs. Advertise that you pick up junk. Then sell it online. One person's packed away stuff is another person's paycheck. Put your basement or garage or barn to use. Build up an inventory of unique items desired by collectors, many of whom are already positioned to survive and prosper during the coming Economic Ice Age and will pay you money.

What do you do at your day job? Become an online consultant in that field nights and weekends. Use a pseudonym if you don't want your boss to know. Are you an attorney? Start an educational service in your area of legal expertise. Are you a CPA? Sell educational services on accounting or simply answer tax questions for a fee. Are you a medical doctor who sold his practice to a big hospital network and are now getting screwed financially – only getting a modest salary that is not commensurate with your education, experience, stress, legal risk, etc.? Do online medical education, providing diagnoses in a question-and-answer format with appropriate legal disclaimers, taking it as far as education but not full diagnosis – for a fee. Yes, for fees. Charge money.

Become a coach. The coaching profession is growing by leaps and bounds, and you can help guide someone into their future. Become a teacher for an online college such as University of Phoenix. Harvard does not have a monopoly on excellence in education. With the right textbooks and a passionate professor with life experience, education, and their own self-taught research, students can get a fabulous education; they can learn to think outside the box at an online school. Convenience and affordability are the wave of the future in education. Online classes will be in greater demand. Hop on now as an adjunct professor at an accredited university.

How about writing a book? Or an ebook? With Amazon.com's Kindle, you can write fifty-page ebooks, self-publish them online, and sell them at Amazon.com and get as much as a couple of dollars per book sold. There are some terrific services online that step you through the publishing process, and ones that design wonderful book covers at very reasonable prices. Write about what you know. Are you a collector of antiquities, baseball cards, comic books, or anything you might find sold in a pawn shop? Write about it and sell it as an ebook. What is your expertise in your day job? Find a different angle, create a fresh approach, and write an ebook about it.

Another way to build cash through a home business is simple family budgeting. Think of it as an ongoing job. Gather everyone together and identify what your family members consider to be luxuries versus necessities. Revisit what are considered necessities to see if they can be recategorized as luxuries. Then cut the portion of your budget spent on items considered luxuries and bank the savings.

Don't be snookered by pyramid sales businesses, in which friends or family or acquaintances from church or the neighborhood are employed by a company to sell a product such as vitamins, vacuum cleaners, or kitchen ware, they hire you as a sales representative under them, and they receive a portion of the commission for the sales you make. If they charge you a fee to join this sales force, it could very likely be a Ponzi scheme. It might sound like a money-maker. You might be given free samples and shown a slick sales pitch at a seminar promising you a free gift. Perhaps you are wined and dined by someone you think you can trust. But if there are no real sales of products going on – if you get a large commission for recruiting other salespeople who must pay a franchise fee to sign up and sell some nifty, packaged, arcane product that hardly ever gets sold – it could be a scam and a way to get a lot of people you see every day very mad at you.

Also be wary of sales positions with outfits that prey on getting a ton of people who really are not good at selling to sell to their close friends and families – a once and done sales party where they use you to sell their product to your close connections – then nothing. Your family and neighbors feel used and you don't have a real, long-lasting job with prospects for other sales. I won't mention names, but we are all familiar with these.

Ordinarily, if the Economic Ice Age were not coming, there is a good chance that the part-time job or business you start or set up for yourself is something you really love, and eventually could replace your full-time day job. But with this trouble coming, it is wise to develop any supplemental source of income, hang on to it for as long as possible, build cash, and pay down debt.

Why? To make yourself your bank. Build up enough cash so that if you need to purchase something you don't need to rely on a credit card or a bank to give you a loan. Lending will be curtailed during this coming economic calamity. Credit card lines will be cut. If you run a small business, do not rely on a bank to give you a line of credit or renew your existing one. Be your own bank. Multiple sources of income can help you build cash balances to become your own bank. Be the lender you need instead of relying on banks. During the coming Economic Ice Age, the old adage will never be truer: "You won't be able to get a loan unless you can prove you do not need it."

Rental income is an excellent extra source of income. Rental income is one of those situations in which your money works for you instead of you working for your money. During the coming period of economic tribulation, it is very likely that real estate values will drop. Buyers will be hard to find because of increasing financial difficulties for the average family, tightened bank lending standards, and because most people do not want to buy something they feel will drop in value. This means the number of people who need to rent or lease real estate will increase. Rental rates should not decline as much as real estate values, and in fact could actually increase over time. You should be able to continue to earn profitable rental income **if you own desirable property**. The best scenario is to own property free and clear near a highly desirable location such as a metropolitan area, a popular vacation resort, or a college. The math works best if you rent a property you owe no debt on. This idea is for those of you who have high net worth on paper – maybe you own significant stock balances. If so, perhaps you should think about rebalancing your assets to include a few rental properties. The caveats include the need for a handyman to do repairs and maintenance, a working knowledge (with the backing of a good attorney) of landlord issues such as tenant rights and lease agreements, with particular attention to lease termination issues. Eviction laws can get messy. To help with this, you can concentrate on rental properties that typically have rotating tenancy, such as apartments near colleges or vacation properties near the beach.

Having three or four sources of income at one time can create some relationship problems with family members. The time it takes to manage multiple incomes can steal from family time. Relationships can suffer and family problems of a non-financial nature can develop. It can be quite a juggling and balancing act. It is going to take a lot of family love and understanding. Good communication is critical. Involving your spouse and children in your work might be a good approach. Making the family part of the decision-making process can help mitigate some of these challenges.

An economic recession or depression puts a lot of stress and strain on families. Not having income or having to work two or three jobs are threats to a full and meaningful life. That is what the markets are saying we are going to be dealing with, and fairly soon. And that is why having large balances of cash will be a huge advantage. Once the cash is built up, you can devote more time to family and give up one of your multiple jobs, buy real estate cheap, rent it out, and let your money work for you while you spend more time with your family. In other words, make the sacrifice, build up cash, then take advantage of buying opportunities, especially in real estate. Become a landlord and enjoy the fruits of your labor. You can do this; you can survive and prosper in the coming Economic Ice Age.

1. www.usdebtclock.org

CHAPTER TEN

Strategy Five: Speculation and Opportunities to Prosper

The first four strategies for surviving and prospering in the coming Economic Ice Age were clearly conservative steps with an aim toward safety, protection, preservation of wealth, and continuity of income. This chapter is a bit outside the box. It focuses on income generation in a more aggressive, yet controlled, disciplined, and high-risk/low-exposure approach.

Whenever there are massive market declines such as we expect in the stock market and which could occur in the fixed-income (federal, municipal and corporate notes and bonds) and real estate markets, there are opportunities to buy at depressed prices – not necessarily bargain prices, but what in the long term certainly could be considered bargain prices. If you have enough cash saved up, enough debt paid down, and have set up three or four independent sources of income, then you will find yourself in a position to take advantage of falling prices and buy stocks, notes, bonds, and real estate cheap. Some of the greatest fortunes ever amassed came by swooping in and buying securities, real estate, businesses, antiquities, and intellectual property that had value at one time but fell because of a falling tide – an overall economic decline during which the owners of these investments were unprepared to hold on to them and had to sell.

This can be a dangerous game, sort of like trying to catch a falling knife in your bare hand. That is because if you buy something that has declined significantly in price and has significantly farther down to go, you bought it at the wrong time – at too high a price. For example, if a house at the beach was going for $1.8 million in 2006 and fell in value to 1.4 million in 2010, and you predict that during the Economic Ice Age it will fall even further to $900,000, you can afford to buy it. But if the market continues to plunge and its value drops to $500,000, you paid too much and put yourself in a bad situation – an illiquid situation, because you cannot sell the property without taking a huge loss. You can hold it hoping the market comes back up, but given the size of the coming Economic Ice Age, you might wait a very long time.

Buying real estate on speculation that the market is nearing a bottom is an amazing opportunity. But it's tricky because of the high price tag of real estate and the need in most cases for financing. If you are sitting on a nest egg of $3.0 million and can be your own bank, you can enter the market at some point to grab a bargain deal with a small percentage of your cash (less than 25 percent since cash is king during an economic depression), but only with the understanding that the amount you invest in that real estate could be tied up for years – essentially money lost for years. Then there is the two-thirds theory, which says that the cost of maintaining and repairing the property, real estate taxes, property insurance, furnishings, etc., will likely cost about a third of the amount of your monthly payment (if your loan doesn't cover taxes and insurance). Another way to look at the two-thirds theory is that you might only be able to afford a property that costs about two-thirds of what you think you can afford. Bad things happen. Expect the best, but prepare for the worst. Be aware that it might not be such a great bargain until the Economic Ice Age is approaching its end.

Buying stocks on speculation is a different animal from buying real estate because you can control the amount you are investing, keep the amount invested small relative to the cost of purchasing property, and play the market to fall, actually benefitting from the decline instead of needing the market to rally in order to make money. Further, you can take advantage of speculative derivative instruments that offer you leverage to generate very high returns if you bet that the price will go in the direction that it does go. There are futures contracts on stocks, and there are options on futures on stocks. There are 3X leveraged ETFs that move in tandem with a stock index such as the Dow 30 Industrials or the S&P 500 and are designed to move three times as much as the stock or stock index itself moves. These derivative instruments are opportunities to take a little of your portfolio, maybe 5 percent maximum, and trade the stock market to go down, then play the typical bounce back in a correction of the decline. There could be a series of these down-up moves throughout the Economic Ice Age, affording you many opportunities to make money on the volatile, oscillating price trends.

What exactly is a derivative? I like Wikipedia's definition:

Derivative is a term that refers to a wide variety of financial instruments whose values are *derived* from one or more underlying assets, market securities or indices. In practice, it is a contract between two parties that specifies conditions (especially the dates), resulting values and definitions of the underlying variables, the parties' contractual obligations, and the notional amount under which payments are to be made between the parties. The most common underlying assets include: commodities, stocks, bonds, interest rates and currencies. Derivatives may broadly be categorized as "lock" or "option" products. Lock products (such as swaps, futures, or forwards) obligate the contractual parties to the terms over the life of the contract. Option products (such as interest rate caps) provide the buyer the right, but not the obligation to enter the contract under the terms specified.

Options or leveraged ETFs are an interesting way to make a little extra money because even if stocks are headed much lower during the Economic Ice Age, they are not going to go straight down. There will be more of a stair-step decline in which prices drop down two levels, then bounce up one, failing to recover the entire previous loss but providing a temporary opportunity to play a rally. Once that rally is over, prices drop down two more levels, then bounce back up one, and so on. Along the way there will probably be a crash or two, meaning we could see a market drop down 20 percent or more very quickly, but if so that means it will be bouncing back up 10 percent or more over a short period of time.

If you follow technical market analysis, such as our service at **www.technicalindicatorindex.com** does, you will see that there are many indicators and pattern signals that give guidance as to when short-term market trend moves are about to change direction, either up or down. If you can time some speculative trading transactions in options or leveraged ETFs to play these moves near their infancy, you can make money as the stock market declines or changes direction and rallies. We cover this in daily and weekend newsletters at our site, and also offer a speculative trading service called our Platinum Trading Program to provide education on possible speculative trades at key turning points in the market.

We typically suggest that no trade be more than 1 percent of your portfolio of cash so that your loss risk is minimal. If you are successful such that you have more wins than losses, you can make a nice little pocket of change. It takes time to learn how to trade options, but if you do paper trading for a while and study the markets and technical indicators and pattern signals we track at our website, it is quite possible to become very successful at trading the derivatives market. Derivatives have a bad reputation in several media circles, as they are difficult to understand; are growing faster than we can get our hands around; and are tied to, but are not in fact, the underlying security instruments bought and sold in cash markets every day. If large banking houses that trade billions and trillions of derivatives do not properly risk-manage their portfolios of derivatives, there is a chance that the entire credit market and banking system can become seriously wounded and, like a house of cards or a line of dominoes, one banking house collapse can bring down another banking house and so on (since they freely trade with and are counterparties to each other), and the entire economy could be decimated.

Today there are over $600 trillion in derivatives in currencies and credit markets. Is this good? Probably not, because of the lack of understanding of this market, its exponential growth and size, and the monumental task of managing its risks. But it is important to understand that derivatives are not inherently bad. They are simply contracts between two parties used to hedge the possibility of a price move in a direction that one of the party's primary businesses cannot benefit from. For example, a farmer who sows a crop of wheat needs assurance that he can sell the crop at harvest time at a price close to the price at planting time. If prices drop between planting and harvesting, the farmer can suffer great financial ruin. The farmer can enter into a derivatives product such as a futures contract that ensures he will get today's price tomorrow. It protects his revenue and assures him of a profit for a relatively small transaction cost.

The problem with the derivatives market is the explosion of its size. In the coming Economic Ice Age there are likely to be defaults on derivatives as counterparty failures occur. If one side of a derivatives trade goes belly up, like Lehman Brothers did in 2008, it can set off a domino effect, toppling a huge chunk of the derivatives market. For example, if you pay $1,000 for a *call option* on the Dow Industrials, playing it to rally, and the rally does occur, and the value of your option rises to $2,000 in a few weeks (yes, that kind of return that fast can happen with options), and you prepare to sell the option but the counterparty to the trade fails to acknowledge the option and goes into default and bankruptcy, you don't get to realize a $1,000 profit and get a $2,000 payout. Instead you lose your entire investment. However, in a smooth-running market this does not happen; you make your profit and cash out, thank you very much.

Options trading can be fun. You can buy an option on a futures contract on most stocks, stock index ETFs, Treasury bonds, commodities, precious metals, and currencies. You simply make a bet, playing the price of the underlying security to rise or to fall between the time you purchase the option and the time it expires. If the security moves in the direction you've bet on, fast or far, you can make a very nice profit on your investment. Further, you can limit the amount you risk based on the number of options you purchase, the time until they expire, or how close their strike prices (the target price you think the security will move toward) are to current prices. The further the price has to move to reach your strike price, the cheaper the cost of the option. You can even make money if your targeted strike price is not achieved but the price of the underlying security you are playing moves substantially in that direction. Then you can sell to close your open position at a higher price than you paid.

There are some great books available that explain the nuances of options trading. I like options if you purchase them long (meaning you are not writing the option and the amount of loss is limited to what you invest, whereas an options writer's risk can be unlimited should the price of the security move very far, very fast). You can buy *call options*, meaning you are playing the underlying security's price to rise, or you can buy *put options*, meaning you are playing it to drop in price. In either case, if the security moves in the direction you are playing, you can make money. Typically the volatility component of a call or put option's price rises when security prices decline, and falls when security prices rise. That is because options writers have more risk when underlying security prices decline because they cannot protect themselves by owning the underlying security the option is playing. Options prices are determined by several component factors including volatility, time to expiration, and its strike price's proximity to the underlying security's (that the option is playing) current market price. If you can find reliable technical buy and sell signals and/or reliable market-trend directional-turn indicators, you can make some very nice money – 20, 50, even 100 percent return or more on your investment. If the market price moves in the opposite direction, the most you will lose is the amount you invested. If you can get three out of every five trades to make money, you can come out ahead. Caution: You do not want to sell options except to close an open position you previously purchased. *Selling naked* means you have unlimited risk of loss.

Options give you the chance to leverage your investment. Let's say you want to play the Dow Industrials 30 stock index to rally. To buy one share of each stock of the entire index would cost you the price of each and every stock added up. It might cost $2,000 to own one share of all 30 stocks. If those stocks rise 2 percent over the next four weeks, your profit would be $40. Peanuts. Less than the commissions would cost you. With options, you might be able to buy ten call options contracts expiring in six weeks for the ETF symbol DIA – which is a close representation of the Dow Industrials stocks – with a targeted strike price 2 percent above today's price, for a total initial investment of $800 ($80 per contract). If the Industrials rally 2 percent over the next month, the value of your options could rise to $200 per contract, for a revenue of $2,000 (ten contracts x $200 per contract) and a profit of $1,200, or 150 percent. Maximum risk to you was $800. The time period for the investment to earn a 150 percent return was one month. Nice. Not all options trades work out this well, especially if market prices move in the opposite direction or do not move much at all during the remaining six weeks of life of the options contract. But if you see a strong trend move coming based on technical market indicators and signals, you can do well. **We provide technical market indicators with buy and sell signals at www.technicalindicatorindex.com.**

I believe that at some point in the Economic Ice Age cycle we will see counterparty failures and trouble in the derivatives market. What the U.S. government might do to shore up the market is the great unknown. Will it step in and make the trades good or will it let the entire derivatives market go down the drain? But I do believe that there will be a solid market for options and futures for a while before danger strikes. I would pay attention to the large money-center banks and investment banking firms. Until a big one goes down, I would be willing to play the speculative options market with a small portion of my cash portfolio. When a big firm does go under, I would see what steps are taken by the government to shore things up. If it looks like the government will support the derivatives market, I would continue to play it with a carefully designed, risk-managed trading portfolio limited to 5 percent of my portfolio. Why? Because money can be made here in a bad economy. I would not bet the farm, would not risk more than 1 percent of my portfolio per trade, and would make sure I knew what I was doing before trading real money.

We are in a low-interest-rate environment. Jobs will be lost, so you need to prepare, educate yourself, and develop the skills necessary to be aggressive and make the money needed to sustain you. It cannot always be done with safe, preservation strategies. You might need to take some risks. **Becoming an options trader can be an interesting self-employment income source.** It is something you can do from home, on the internet.

CHAPTER ELEVEN

Positioning Your Portfolio: A Conservative, Balanced Investment Portfolio Model

Below is a conservative, balanced investment portfolio model from January 1st, 2013. You can start something similar at any time before the Economic Ice Age begins. This model is designed to protect wealth and make money during the economic crisis that I expect to start sometime in 2014 or 2015 and last through 2020 or 2022.

The last time I designed a conservative portfolio was October of 2006, and I made it available to our market services subscribers at **www.technicalindicatorindex.com**. I saw an economic crisis coming that in fact did occur from 2007 through 2009. I wrote about that coming economic collapse on my website and in articles I posted at **www.safehaven.com** and **www.gold-eagle. com** many months before it occurred. That conservative portfolio outperformed the S&P 500 by 54 percent over the following five years, from 2007 through 2011. It increased in value by 30 percent during a time when the stock market fell 50 percent. The $500,000 portfolio grew to $650,000 over the five years from 2006 to 2011, when interest rates fell to close to zero percent. This extraordinary performance was accomplished by investing conservatively, as discussed in chapters six through eight, and using a small element of aggressive and speculative trading as was covered in chapter ten. In other words, the theories and suggestions I present in this book were tested and proven during the Great Recession of 2007 through 2009. Each person's risk appetite, experience, and financial position are different, so you can certainly tweak the model I have set up for you in this chapter to suit your unique circumstances. You can always take on more risk than this model suggests.

Just as I saw a coming economic collapse back in late 2006, which arrived the next year, I now see an even greater economic collapse in our future. This time the economic decline will be worse than we have seen in a century – worse than the declines of 2000 to 2002 and 2007 to 2009, and more ominous than in the 1930s. It has the potential to be the mother of all economic collapses. It could be a period of great tribulation. I've provided a new conservative portfolio model designed to survive the coming collapse, protect wealth, and make some money during a time when income will be very hard to come by.

What follows is an initial investment portfolio – a starting point – including a schedule of initial transactions. At my website, **www.technicalindicatorindex.com,** I have posted a similar portfolio model, and I add transactions to that from time to time. If you would like to follow this conservative portfolio model dynamically, my team and I provide appropriate revisions as part of the services for our subscribers. We update this portfolio with current market values as of future reporting dates. We also conduct new transactions from time to time, build the portfolio for a declining economy, and make adjustments necessary to weather the storm. The accounting is on a cash basis.

I start the portfolio heavy with cash and a plan to put that cash to work over time, some of it more quickly than the rest. I have targeted allocations in gold and Treasury bills and notes in a laddered maturity structure (see chapter eight), and will eventually add some minor holdings in a "Buy and Hold Equity" portfolio. I will explain how that works later in this chapter. I might add to the Buy and Hold Equity portfolio using a dollar-cost-averaging strategy (which I will also cover later in this chapter) on a periodic basis, but on a limited basis, keeping the allocation to buy and hold at only 5 to 10 percent of the entire portfolio. The Buy and Hold Equity portfolio might include ETFs, playing markets to decline. The "Market-Timing Stocks" segment of the portfolio, limited to 10 percent of the portfolio, includes a diversification of short (bear) fund and long (bull) fund ETFs including leveraged funds and ETFs designed to move two or three times the distance of the movement of cash stock markets (playing stocks to fall or rise), precious metals such as gold and silver, and mining stocks. The "Market Speculation" portion of the portfolio uses options trades with appropriate risk-management limitations. I keep my cash only at FDIC-insured financial institutions and in money-market accounts that provide reasonable interest rates for safety and yield and a place to park funds until put to use. Again, this is a conservative portfolio. A more aggressive portfolio would hold more stocks than this portfolio does, and may outperform in some areas while underperforming in others. But that is not what this portfolio is all about. This is for those who do not like risk but need returns greater than FDIC-insured deposit accounts provide.

One of the challenges in starting a new portfolio at this time is that we are in an environment in which Treasury bill yields remain near zero percent and FDIC-insured money-market cash yields remain low at 0.10 percent. So I want to be careful not to take risk with weak-credit-rated commercial notes or junk bonds to capture tempting higher yields that could end up destroying principal (the amount invested) should the issuers go bankrupt. There is also the possibility that interest rates will rise as U.S. and world sovereign debts rise, default, or become monetized by excessive printing of currencies. This portfolio starts out with very-short-term Treasury investments.

I choose U.S. Treasury bills and notes rather than other sovereign, municipal, or commercial fixed-income securities because I believe the coming economic decline could lead to world war and that currency and debt instruments should be held in the nation that has the strongest military and most stable political structure. As I said above, in my opinion, that is the United States of America. Major companies doing well now could face bankruptcy as the economy slips into recession and eventual depression. There might not be "too big to fail" rescues during the Economic Ice Age as were seen from the government in the past, because government budgets will be strained and there might not be the political will to bail out large banks and corporations. You do not want to be holding corporate debt in such an environment. Municipal securities have tax risk as Congress is tempted to change the income tax structure to deal with this coming decline. Further, local and state municipalities will come under increasing credit risk as they strain to manage budgets due to declining tax revenues as the economy worsens. Regardless of what the major credit-rating agencies such as S&P and Moody's and Fitch decide to rate U.S. Treasuries, I feel Treasuries will be as good a credit risk as there will be on the planet besides gold and silver.

If war drums start to beat, I might add a defense sector ETF, or perhaps buy some of the major component stocks, placing them in the market-timing segment of the portfolio. One such ETF might be ITA, an iShares Dow Jones U.S. Aerospace and Defense ETF. I am not advocating this particular ETF, just mentioning it as one of several possible ways to invest in the defense sector once war approaches. You will want to do your own due diligence, perhaps with the help of an investment advisor, before choosing an ETF.

This conservative portfolio model includes no Madoff funds, no high-risk stuff, no wipeout-of-life-savings Ponzi-scheme instruments. It advocates basic, high-quality securities and returns. I choose to take an extreme conservative posture for 2014 and beyond based on several risk factors I see in technical market indicators and patterns, warning that economic trouble is approaching – the sort of trouble that will be very hard for governments to mitigate and fix.

The model includes a small speculative element that plays the options market, with strategies discussed in chapter ten, which is our **Platinum Trading Program,** an educational service offered to subscribers by Main Line Investors, Inc. at the website **www. technicalindicatorindex.com**. But that risk is limited to less than 5 percent of this total portfolio, and each transaction is usually less than 1 percent of the portfolio in keeping with the portfolio's conservative theme. While I expect to invest heavily in cash, precious metals, and Treasuries, I plan to enhance yield by conducting speculative trades in the Platinum Trading Program while also conducting several market-timing trades during periods of high-probability trends, both up and down, including ETFs that manage leveraged long (bull) and short (bear) positions. Once risks subside, and that might not be for several more years, I plan to move from an *extreme* conservative posture to a conservative posture, meaning I will likely add more equities to the portfolio and reduce cash holdings.

Some basic theory regarding this portfolio is presented at the end of this chapter. I update this portfolio model periodically, with comments on decisions made, and publish those transactions at the "Conservative Portfolio Transactions" button at the home page at **www.technicalindicatorindex.com**, and publish speculative trades for the Platinum Trading Program (see chapter ten) at the "Platinum Archives" button at the home page. Not all days see transaction activity. The portfolio's aim is overall return within the constraints of wealth preservation and liquidity. It must be safe and offer satisfactory returns potential and liquidity in most economic environments. Platinum Trading Program speculative trades are carefully risk-managed. In catastrophic economic times, I look primarily for wealth preservation and liquidity.

Conservative Balanced Investment Portfolio Model
Initial Portfolio Value $500,000 1/2/2013

As of January 1st, 2013

Category: (Cash Basis Accounting)

A. Cash and Cash Equivalents (Unallocated):

	Date Acquired	Cost Basis Investment	Value at Maturity	Maturity	Coupon	Yield	Market Value
	1/2/2013						
FDIC Insured Moneymarket		$ 200,010.87	$ 200,010.87			0.10%	$ 200,010.87

B. Gold (Target Portfolio Allocation 10 Percent)

		Cost Basis Investment	Value at Maturity			Yield	
Cash		$50,133.00	$50,133.00			0.10%	

	Date Acquired	Cost Basis Investment					Market Value
15 Ounces at 1,657.80	1/2/2013	$ 24,867.00					$ 24,867.00
Subtotal		$75,000.00					$75,000.00

C. U.S. Treasury Bills, Notes, and Bonds (Target Portfolio Allocation 40 Percent)

	Date	Cost Basis	Value at				Market

	Acquired	Investment	Maturity	Maturity	Coupon	Yield	Value
Treasury Bills	1/2/2013	$ 134,981.51	$ 135,000.00	12/12/2013	0.000%	0.137%	$ 134,981.51
Treasury Note	1/2/2013	$ 15,007.62	$ 15,000.00	6/30/2014	0.250%	0.219%	$ 15,007.62
Subtotal Bill, Notes, & Bonds		$ 149,989.13	$ 150,000.00			0.15%	$ 149,989.13

D. Stocks Buy and Hold Dollar Cost Averaging (Target Portfolio Allocation 10 Percent)

	Cost Basis Investment	Value at Maturity		Yield	Market Value
Cash	$25,000	$25,000		0.10%	

	Date Acquired	Cost Basis Investment	Number of Shares	Price Per Share		Market Value
SDOW Proshares 3x Leveraged Short Dow 30		$ -	0	0		$ -
Dow Industrials ETF DIA		$ -	0	0		$ -
S&P 500 ETF SPY		$ -				
NASDAQ 100 ETF QQQQ		$ -	0	0		$ -
Russell 2000 ETF IWM		$ -				
HUI Amex Gold Bugs ETF GDX		$ -	0	0		$ -
Subtotal Buy & Hold Portfolio		$25,000.00				$25,000.00

E. Market-Timing Stocks (Target Portfolio Allocation 5 Percent)

	Date Acquired	Cost Basis Investment	Value at Maturity	Maturity	Coupon	Yield	Market Value
Cash		$19,114.00	$19,114.00			0.10%	$19,114.00

	Date Acquired	Cost Basis Investment	Number of Shares	Price Per Share			Market Value
UDOW Proshares 3x Leveraged Bull Dow 30							
	1/4/2013	$ 5,886.00	100	58.86			$ 5,886.00
Dow Industrials ETF DIA		$ -	0	0			$ -
S&P 500 ETF SPY							
NASDAQ 100 ETF QQQQ		$ -	0	0			$ -
Russell 2000 ETF IWM							
HUI Amex Gold Bugs ETF GDX		$ -	0	$ -			$ -
Australia SPASX200		$ -	0	$ -			$ -
SILVER ETF SLV		$ -	0	0			$ -
Subtotal Non-cash Holdings		$ -					
Subtotal Market Timing Portfolio		$25,000.00					$25,000.00

F. Market Speculation -- Trader's Corner (Target Portflio Allocation 5 Percent)

	Date Acquired	Cost Basis Investment	Value at Maturity	Maturity	Coupon	Yield	Market Value
Cash		$25,000	$25,000			0.10%	$25,000

Options	Date Acquired	Cost Basis Investment	Price Per Contract	Expiration	Strike Price	# of Contracts	Market Value
		$0.00	$ -		0	-	$ -

Subtotal Market Speculation Portfolio	$25,000		$25,000

Portfolio Summary:

Cash	$ 200,010.87		$ 200,010.87
Gold	$ 75,000.00		$ 75,000.00
Treasuries	$ 149,989.13		$ 149,989.13
Stocks - Buy and Hold	$ 25,000.00		$ 25,000.00
Stocks - Market Timing	$ 25,000.00		$ 25,000.00
Speculative Holdings	$ 25,000.00		$ 25,000
Total	$ 500,000.00		$ 500,000.00

Transactions Since Opening January 2nd, 2013:

1. Purchased gold with 5 percent of the portfolio, and plan to add more up to a 15 percent position.

2. Placed 30 percent of the portfolio in very-short-term Treasury bills and notes. As interest rates rise, I will replace maturing bills and notes with a ladder portfolio, gradually extending the maturities, edging them longer as rates rise.

3. Purchased 100 shares of UDOW, a 3X leveraged Proshares ETF designed to play the Dow 30 Industrials to rally from 1/4/13. This trade is playing the final rally leg for the Jaws of Death pattern.

4. The balance is in cash at this time. Will add positions in SDOW short ETF fund for the Dow Industrials, and perhaps for other major stock indices once the Jaws of Death is complete.

5. Will add a defense sector ETF such as ITA in case of war.

6. Will play speculative call and put options in our Platinum Trading Program with the speculative segment of the portfolio to enhance overall portfolio yield.

7. In the "Timing" segment of the portfolio, will play both rising and falling trends as stocks stair-step lower, relying on buy and sell signals at www.technicalindicatorindex.com for timing.

One of the problems with publishing one conservative portfolio model is that there is no such thing as a one-size-fits-all portfolio or portfolio strategy. However, as an education service to our many subscribers, I run a paper portfolio (where theoretical transactions occur that track actual investments, but without having to actually invest the cash – a trading simulation learning tool) that includes several elements of a balanced portfolio but leans toward the conservative. It offers several segments with different objectives such as diversification, liquidity, earnings, capital gains, and speculative profits – again, for educational purposes. If you are interested, read on as we discuss the theoretical makeup of this portfolio.

First, procedure. I present a start-up investment portfolio as if I had inherited, picked up in a windfall, or built up over time a savings portfolio or 401(k) in the amount of $500,000 as of January 1st, 2013, and need to manage this money. The portfolio's aim is overall return within the constraints of wealth preservation and liquidity. It must be relatively safe and offer strong returns -potential and liquidity in most economic environments. It is weighted heavily in cash at the onset, and then over time puts the cash to work in a variety of ways. I publish all transactions as they are performed, even daily if the portfolio is worked that hard, and periodically publish the latest portfolio inventory which can be compared with the original starting position, available in the "Guest Articles" section at www.technicalindicatorindex.com.

While fictitious, the model uses actual investments and actual pricing, and operates in real time as much as possible given this forum. It is not to be construed as trading advice, but rather is educational in nature, perhaps entertaining, and hopefully idea-generating and informative. Investment segment allocations can be altered based on your risk appetite, investment experience, and financial position. It is not intended to be a financial plan, as that would include life insurance, real estate, and estate and tax planning. This conservative, balanced portfolio would be just a piece of your financial-plan pie, nothing more.

The portfolio does not get heavy into tax-planning vehicles, except maybe on occasion to add some federal-tax-free instruments (municipal securities) if I happen to like the risk/reward. If so, total return will be computed on a tax-equivalent basis. As noted in chapter eight, during the coming Economic Ice Age there will be increasing credit risk, and possible legislative tax risk, in owning municipals, which means I am likely to stay away from them once the economic collapse begins. The model does not deal with transaction costs in order to simplify the accounting, but understand that every transaction has costs, broker fees, etc. Typically online brokerage fees are minor and in most cases immaterial. This portfolio model is a plain and simple approach for idea-generation in a real-time setting with real investments with a conservative leaning. Every investment advisor has their own preferences in investment vehicles, strategies, etc., so don't be surprised by independent reviews that are critical of this model. So be it. This is just one approach that I feel is of interest to a broad spectrum of investors. Everyone is different, and if you were to apply any of this portfolio management to your own unique circumstances, no doubt you'd tweak what I have here to be more suitable to your needs, which is great. **Before you follow anything in this portfolio, I suggest you check with your financial advisor first**.

This portfolio's management is dynamic, meaning active. Long-term strategies will likely change with the times, possibly forfeiting returns now for higher returns later. A perfect example of that is all the cash I've started out with. The portfolio has segments that utilize the key trend-finder indicator buy and sell signals provided at **www.technicalindicatorindex.com**, and has segments that do not market-time but are more buy and hold. I like cash. That won't excite everyone, but part of running a conservative portfolio is the wisdom to be prepared for future opportunities for which you would need cash.

Following are the six segments of the conservative, balanced portfolio model and some basic theory for each:

Segment A: Cash

The purpose of cash is for emergency liquidity and to be in a position to seize future opportunities. The portfolio uses primarily FDIC-insured money-market funds. Return is a minor consideration here. Initially the portfolio has a large cash position that is eventually put to work.

Segment B: Gold

The purpose of holding gold is for protection against inflation, against a debasement of our currency, and as catastrophe insurance (in case of natural disasters or pestilence on a grand scale, political change, or war). The portfolio accumulates ounces of the metal in either coins or a gold ETF. Gold is measured using the daily spot prices for simplicity.

Segment C: U.S. Treasury Bills, Notes, and Bonds

These are safe havens that are alternatives to cash, and once interest rates rise they are strong contributors to overall portfolio yield. I chose a laddered selection of maturities that provides safety for your principal (the amount you invest) – as close to risk-free as possible, a continuous flow of liquidity, and potential capital gains – probably about every three years – that improve long-term total return. The ladder resembles a barbell from time to time, depending on the economy and the interest-rate cycle. This strategy is laid out in detail in chapter eight.

Segment D: Stocks and ETF Funds – Buy and Hold

Here the portfolio might employ a ***dollar-cost-averaging*** strategy for long-term capital gains, but only after considering the economic risks that stocks bear. I might include some consideration of dividend yield as a component of decision-making, but for the most part will trade index ETFs – not individual stocks but rather indices (such as DIAs for the Dow Industrials, SPY for the S&P 500, IWM for the small caps Russell 2000, or QQQs for the NASDAQ 100), because we are dealing with a coming tide of economic calamity that should affect most stocks. I prefer to trade large sectors that will move in tandem with the tide. Different sectors of the broad equity market are selected depending on whether one sector is favored over another.

So how does ***dollar-cost-averaging*** work? Essentially, a minimum amount of dollars worth of stock is purchased periodically, with the same amount of money invested each time and the quantity of stock being purchased varying depending on what prices do. For example, maybe I decide to invest $1,000 the last day of every month. If prices rise next month, I will be buying less quantity for my $1,000, but I am happy because my original investment rose in value. If prices fall next month, I will be happy because I am able to buy more shares of the stock for the same $1,000. This is a time-tested strategy that works best in either volatile markets or long-term rising markets. The idea here is that when prices drop, you get to buy more quantity for the same dollars in the short run, and because you have a larger quantity of stocks as the economic decline continues, once the stock market goes back up and prices start to rise again, the value of your portfolio of stocks grows exponentially at the next real bull market. It is basically what is going on with 401(k) plans, where the same amount is withdrawn from each paycheck and invested in the market. Dividend-paying stocks fit here. As a new wrinkle, you can even add short (bear) funds or ETFs that gain in value as stock prices fall, given the long period of time I expect this coming economic collapse to last. In this case, as the stock market rises, the quantity of short (bear) ETFs will increase since I am investing the same dollars at cheaper prices (bear funds decline as the stock market rises and rise as the stock market declines). However, as the stock market declines, that increasing quantity of bear-fund ETF shares will rise significantly in value.

Segment E: Stocks – Market Timing

This is a more aggressive strategy that is capital-gains-focused. Using the key trend-finder indicator buy and sell signals at **www.technicalindicatorindex. com**, I can add to long positions in stock index ETFs when the key trend-finder indicators generate new buy signals, and increase cash (do not short) when either hitting a target profit objective or when new sell signals are generated. I might not go to all cash when sells are given, but will increase cash. Or, if you want to play the decline, you can choose to purchase short-fund (bear) ETFs that are designed to increase in value when the stock market is expected to decline such as SDOW (a Proshares 3X leveraged ETF playing the Dow 30 Industrials to decline), or bull-fund ETFs when the stock market is expected to rally such as UDOW (a Proshares 3X leveraged ETF designed to rally when the stock market rallies). I am not advocating these two ETFs, just mentioning them as possibilities for educational purposes. *Shorting* means you are agreeing to sell a security in the future at today's prices – a security that you do not own today and will have to buy tomorrow to fulfill this agreement to sell. In essence you are betting that the price of the security will decline in the future, below today's price, allowing you to buy it at a lower price later, in which case you make money. You buy it in the future at a lower price and get to sell it at today's higher price. If prices rise instead of decline, you lose. Buying *put options* or bear funds accomplishes this shorting for you.

Segment F: Market Speculation (Platinum Trading Program)

This is essentially the Platinum Trading Program from Main Line Investors, Inc. at **www.technicalindicatorindex.com**, an educational service where an investor can speculate in non-cash instruments such as stock index put or call options in which the investor can leverage investment returns, but at high risk. The full body of technical market analysis covered in newsletters at **www.technicalindicatorindex.com** is used while I make speculative trades with a very small percentage of the entire portfolio, with an aim of generating large gains from time to time by both going long (buying calls) and going short (buying puts). This strategy does not write or sell uncovered options, as this is a conservative portfolio and those are not conservative strategies. Writing *covered calls* (where you already own the security and the option being purchased from you gives the buyer the right to take from you should its price rise to a certain level) is considered acceptable for this segment, but is not used for the sake of simplicity. Heavy reliance is placed on the use of our key trend-finder indicator buy and sell signals.

Initial target allocations are 30 percent bills, notes, and bonds; 15 percent gold; zero percent stocks – buy and hold; 5 percent market timing; and 5 percent speculation; with the remainder in cash. This allocation will likely change over time depending on where risks and opportunities are seen.

Periodic updated inventories of this portfolio are posted regularly as the conservative portfolio model is revised over time, available in the "Conservative Portfolio Model" section at **www.technicalindicatorindex.com**.

This is not trading advice, merely a fictitious educational model that uses real-time real investment data to model a conservative, balanced portfolio with the objective of safety, liquidity, and total return for the coming Economic Ice Age environment.

CHAPTER TWELVE

Is There a Chance that the Economic Ice Age Can Be Averted?

Great question. To quote Charles Dickens's *A Christmas Carol*:

> "Answer me one question. Are these the shadows of the things that *will* be, or are they shadows of things that *may* be, only?" Still the Ghost pointed downward to the grave by which it stood. "Men's courses will foreshadow certain ends, to which, if persevered in, they must lead," said Scrooge. "But if the courses be departed from, the ends will change. Say it is thus with what you show me!"

There is always the possibility that the Economic Ice Age can be averted. But based on the history and reliability of the Jaws of Death pattern, it would take Divine intervention to prevent the coming economic collapse. The Old Testament is filled with stories of how men moved God to stop disaster. But it is also filled with stories in which disaster was forewarned and occurred for cleansing, for renewal.

Let's start with a study of the reliability of the Jaws of Death pattern. As discussed above, in technical market analysis textbooks this pattern is commonly known as the megaphone pattern. It can appear at either tops or bottoms and represents turning points in the market. This pattern appears when the trend heading into it is about to reverse. In the present case, the megaphone, or Jaws of Death pattern (I have so dubbed it because it looks like a shark's mouth, wide open, ready to devour its prey), is clearly a top. No doubt about that. So it means we are talking about a trend turn from up to down. Not good.

What is happening psychologically in a megaphone top, or a Jaws of Death top? The broadening formation that accompanies this pattern is decompression, creating a series of higher highs and lower lows. It is telling us that participants in the market are becoming less and less certain about what the correct valuation for the stock market should be. It almost always leads to a directional trend reversal from the direction in which prices were headed before the pattern started. The pattern we are watching now started in 1990. The stock market had been rising for almost 300 years (starting in Europe before the United States came into existence) heading into the start of this Jaws of Death pattern. The message of the market is that stocks are going to reverse their course from the past 300 years, which was up, and head down. The decline will be huge because the 300-year rally was huge and because the pattern is the largest we have ever seen – twenty-three years in the making so far – as opposed to just a year or two as seen in the eight prior instances in which it appeared over the past 100 years.

In Thomas N. Bulkowski's excellent technical market analysis book, *Encyclopedia of Chart Patterns* (John Wiley & Sons, Inc., copyright 2000), he tells us that the statistical probability of this pattern failing is a very low 4 percent. That means the chances of a trend reversal down once this pattern completes is 96 percent. This is one highly reliable pattern, unfortunately. It is a five-point reversal pattern, and where we are now is near the very end of the fifth and final point (which I labeled in the chart for the Jaws of Death pattern in chapter one as point (E)).

Once the reversal occurs – once the fifth and final top point is reached – the downside target is at least to the lowest point in the pattern, which was point (D), or the 2009 low in the Industrials. However, there is a very good chance that prices will fall below the extended bottom boundary for this pattern, meaning we could see the Industrials fall below their March 9th, 2009, closing low of 6,547, and the S&P 500 could fall below its 676 closing low on March 9th, 2009. Based on the size of this pattern, and on the amount of time it is correcting – over 300 years of Grand Supercycle rally – I expect stocks to fall significantly below those March 2009 levels. We have seen a drop below the bottom boundary point (D) in the Jaws of Death pattern happen before.

The eight previous Jaws of Death patterns I cite in chapter one all resulted in strong reversal declines. Eight for eight. Again, this is a reliable pattern.

Is there a chance that the pattern will blow up, meaning the symmetry of the pattern diverges from the textbook pattern it is forming? The pattern is nearly complete, so there is very little chance for it to metamorphose into something different than the Jaws of Death. The final wave (E) rally for this pattern is about 90 percent complete. Here is the thing: If prices continue to rise from here, the rise will fulfill the pattern as it reaches the upper boundary. If prices fall from here and do not reach the upper boundary, that does not invalidate the pattern because 90 percent of the final-leg higher has been completed, and a decline from here would simply be what is called a *truncation*. Truncations occur when the power behind the coming trend turn is so strong that the reversal starts early. It is as if the coming economic collapse is anxious to get started. The odds favor prices rising to the upper boundary before reversing, and at this point this pattern looks very close to completion and is of textbook quality.

With these odds, we need to prepare as if the Economic Ice Age is a virtual certainty.

In chapter five, "The Sabotaging of the American Economy," I showed how politicians and Federal Reserve policymakers failed us, feeding this monster pattern and fulfilling its development. I believe we had an opportunity to change the outcome as this pattern was developing, but failed to take the necessary steps to prevent its formation. Now we sit very close to its concluding moments, and to stop it now would take a miracle.

If government policymakers were to try to avert the coming disaster, they would be acting from a very wounded position – a position of great weakness. With the massive U.S. deficit, out-of-control debt, and astronomical unfunded liabilities, it is a bad spot to start out from. To quote a famous philosopher shining his basket of eggs in the movie **Funny Farm** (Warner Brothers, 1988), when a couple of lost out-of-towners try unsuccessfully to find Red Bud, a small obscure town in New England, this wise and helpful man responded simply, "Well if I were going there, I sure as hell wouldn't start from here." Precisely.

But what if we had to? What can we, as a nation, possibly do now?

Let's explore for a moment, fundamentally, what it would take for that 4 percent chance that an economic collapse can be averted – for the Jaws of Death pattern not to be prescient. Our total economic pie would need to grow, grow fast, and outgrow our economic problems. In other words, we would need record growth in Gross Domestic Product. How does that happen under the strained economic conditions this economy faces? It would take the most sensational government intervention in markets and the economy of all time, with the caveat that it would have to be the most sensational *correct* strategy and tactics of intervention. If you accelerate the speed of a powerful train you are riding on, it does not get you closer to your desired destination if it is running on the wrong track.

It would take a huge change in economic philosophy from what we have seen over the past twelve years. The economy has been managed top-down, with almost all stimulus aimed at the top end of the market – Wall Street – in the hope that benefits and economic growth will trickle down to Main Street. This approach has been an abject failure. Unemployment remains terrible, housing remains frozen, confidence in markets is poor, savings remain low, debt remains out of control, and inflation of necessities (products and services such as gasoline, education, medicine, and food) has risen while sectors such as real estate have seen price erosion. In the United States we have seen a weird mix of top-down infusion of economic stimulus to Wall Street, entitlement escalation, and wealth redistribution. Not working.

The focus of U.S. government has been on wealth redistribution as we just saw in the Fiscal Cliff resolution January 1st, 2013. Wealth redistribution is a form of socialism. That economic philosophy was tried in the 1900s in communist China and the Soviet Union, among other nations. Socialism such as we see in southern Europe does not work today, where entitlements (government handouts including jobs, health insurance, and pensions) have exploded. The sovereign nation economies of Spain, Portugal, Italy, and Greece are essentially bankrupt, with a consequent strain on northern Europe. We can see the tip of the glacier – of the Economic Ice Age – approaching in clear view in Europe. We are skating on fragile ice.

The U.S. economy is a like a skier racing down a mountain with an avalanche fast on his heels, gaining on him. Think about this: The Federal Reserve's balance sheet has increased by $4.0 trillion over the past four years, almost all of it securities purchased from Wall Street in exchange for newly printed dollars sent back to Wall Street, and essentially none of it given to Main Street America – U.S. households and small businesses. This has been very bad policy and has done nothing to grow our economic pie, which has to happen in a big way to grow ourselves out of this massive debt problem and avert the coming economic disaster of which the Jaws of Death pattern forewarns.

Honestly, with only a 4 percent chance that the pattern fails and an economic collapse does not come, we certainly need to prepare. If we believe the skier is about to be buried in snow, if the Economic Ice Age is unstoppable, maybe it would make sense to take the risky step that I explain below in the hope that it gives the economy such a shot of adrenaline – such a steroid injection – that it shocks the economy into double-digit GDP growth for the next five to ten years. We just might be able to helicopter that skier out of harm's way, lift him above the plunging ice and snow, and try to save his life. The idea is highly risky because it requires that the U.S. government add a ton of debt at one time, in effect changing the direction of the avalanche by dropping a bomb ahead of it, resulting in a wall of snow that acts as a barrier protecting our skier. Think of it as treating the disease with the disease, but attacking it in a different way than has been occurring since the year 2000.

Here is the mother of all government intervention strategies to grow the economic pie at an unprecedented speed, and soon: The U.S. Treasury could issue $5.0 trillion in new securities and sell them to the Federal Reserve for $5.0 trillion in U.S. dollars. The Treasury could then issue a massive income tax rebate across the board to all households and small businesses, refunding the past two years of income taxes paid, with a minimum rebate of $50,000 per household and small business.

The recipients – households and small businesses – would be required to pay off debt with at least half the rebate. They can do whatever they want to with the other half. Presumably they will spend most of the other half.

What will be the result of this? Consumer spending will increase, which will boost demand for small-business goods and services, which will increase demand for the products that large corporations provide to small businesses, which will boost the need for Wall Street capital for large corporations that suddenly find their businesses growing. It will increase the need for small businesses to hire more people in both low- and high-wage positions as demand for their products and services increases their need to expand.

Another benefit would be that a large chunk of banks' loan assets (both good and non-performing loans) will be paid off via the mandatory payments required as part of the rebate program, reducing their portfolios of underperforming loans and reducing their revenues from loans, giving them the incentive to be more accommodative and to lend, opening up the housing and real estate industry and increasing working capital for small businesses.

Further, I would pass legislation that requires the Federal government to guarantee to the lending bank 15 percent of the purchase price of every real estate property, meaning the required down payment for real estate would drop from the currently unachievable 20 percent to a far more achievable 5 percent. Construction would increase, jobs would increase, and property values would rise. As banks' loans are paid down with the income tax rebate, bank risk-based capital levels would rise since loans require more capital than securities on a bank's balance sheet, thereby strengthening the nation's financial institutions.

The overall result would be a massive stimulus to the economy and a huge boost in the growth of GDP. And here is the interesting part: a boost in taxable income. This means federal, state, and local governments could keep tax rates the same or reduce them, and their tax receipts would increase, which can be used to reduce deficits, reduce debt, fund infrastructure projects, etc. I would go a step further. I would reduce the federal income tax rate to 10 percent across the board, or eliminate it completely and replace it with a national consumption sales tax. The lower taxes are, the more money everyone gets to keep, which boosts economic growth.

The increase in tax revenues coming from taxing a much larger economic pie (a result of the accelerated growth in the economy) can be used to pay off the $5.0 trillion in Treasury securities issued to the Fed to finance the income tax rebate. Voilà.

If the government were to institute the above plan, but only to a quarter of the degree – perhaps with a significant but smaller income tax rebate and rate reduction, the likely outcome would be that the coming plunge would be delayed, but not averted. The stock market would crawl along the upper boundary of the Jaws of Death pattern for a few more years before the plunge arrived, kicking off the economic collapse. The Jaws of Death pattern would prove accurate, but take more time to complete. The Economic Ice Age is a question of when, not if. What we have seen time and time again is government kicking the can down the road, foregoing pain, passing the trouble down to the next generation. Time is running out, even if the government intervenes again. Each QE program the Fed has introduced over the past five years has had diminishing returns.

Here is the reality that the Jaws of Death is telling us with 96 percent certainty: Politics and the tendency for the status quo to perpetuate itself will prevent the solution I propose, which means we are going into the Economic Ice Age. The Jaws of Death stock price pattern will prove accurate, and we need to prepare by following the proactive steps outlined in chapters six through ten. If we do, we will survive and actually have the opportunity to prosper.

The coming Economic Ice Age will present amazing opportunities for those who are prepared. Preparation is key. There was a meteorological ice age that struck Europe between 1500 and 1800 AD. The cold weather wiped out many grain crops, causing food shortages and necessitating a change in farming. The solution was to farm underground foods such as the potato; an opportunity came along that lives on today. We are going to have to prepare, adapt, and identify new opportunities for survival and prosperity. Those opportunities will come along with the trouble. You want to be in position to seize those opportunities.

One last thought. If you prepare for the coming Economic Ice Age, and it does not come by some miracle, you will be in a stronger financial position because you took the steps to prepare. You can be thankful and enjoy the fruits of your efforts and a new prosperity.

"For I know the plans I have for you," declares the LORD,

"plans to prosper you and not to harm you,

plans to give you hope and a future."

Jeremiah 29:11

About the Author

Dr. Robert McHugh is President and CEO of Main Line Investors, Inc., which is located at **www.technicalindicatorindex.com**. Main Line Investors, Inc. is a market forecasting, investment, and trading education firm servicing both institutional and private investors globally. Dr. McHugh provides a daily and expanded weekend report forecasting trends in stock, precious metal, currency, oil, and bond markets. His firm also provides both conservative model portfolios and **a unique educational Platinum Trading Program, a speculative trading program to help investors make money in both rising** *and falling markets.*

Dr. McHugh is the originator of several key market forecasting buy and sell indicators that are only available for his subscribers, and that have helped steer them through the dangerous waters of 2007 through 2009 (he accurately predicted the stock market crash of 2008) and guided them to wealth-building and financial prosperity during the stock bull market since 2009. Now he once again is warning that economic trouble is ahead and that it is time to prepare.

Dr. McHugh has a Ph.D. in finance and an MBA. He has taught graduate degree finance at the university level. He began his career in banking, and was chief investment officer and chief financial officer of two of the largest regional banks in the U.S. He is the author of numerous financial articles in leading magazines and is a contributing author at several financial websites. He has testified before the U.S. Congress on Federal Reserve matters. He resides outside Philadelphia, Pennsylvania, with his wife and two children.

Acknowledgements

First and foremost, I want to mention my wonderful, intelligent, and wise wife, Denise, for essentially being the executive producer of this project. From inspiring me to write this important message to editing the raw manuscript, finding me the right publisher, designing the cover, and spearheading the marketing and promotion, this book is as much yours as it is mine – thank you. Thank you for putting aside the books you are writing so this time-sensitive project would come first. This book would not have happened without you, my best friend. You have believed in me through thick and thin.

Thanks to my son, Daniel (Buddy), for editing the manuscript just before entering law school. Thanks to my daughter, Shawna, for giving up time with Mom and Dad so this book could happen.

I would also like to acknowledge Lynne Klippel, my editor and publisher at Thomas Noble Books, www.BusinessBuildingBooks.com, who worked tirelessly on this book and enthusiastically saw its importance and potential. Gwen Hoffnagle did a masterful job with the final editing and proofing.

Thanks to John Engel for the fabulous technology support behind my website. Thanks to Todd Shill, Esq. and Kevin Gold, Esq. for handling the business of copyrights and trademarks.

Thanks also to my many loyal subscribers who read what I write and send me email after email showing a hunger for my work and encouraging me to continue with the challenge of forecasting the markets.

For Assistance with Your Financial Future

If you are interested in learning more about where markets are headed; if you want the investing advantage, simply go to **www.technicalindicatorindex.com** and check out Main Line Investors, Inc.'s reports, articles, and services, including **a Free 30-day Trial Subscription** to our daily and weekend market reports, forecasting stocks, precious metals, currencies, oil, and bonds as the coming Economic Ice Age approaches.

We offer an educational **Platinum Trading Program** for those who are interested in independently managing a speculative trading program within a portion of their portfolio. You can send an email to Dr. McHugh at **mainrdmch@aol.com** for information on the Platinum Trading Program.

NARDHEIM.

Made in the USA
Lexington, KY
18 December 2013

28419419R00087